VICTORIA AND ALBERT

A Family Life at Osborne House

HRH THE DUCHESS OF YORK

— WITH —

BENITA STONEY

PRENTICE
HALL
PRESS

New York · London · Toronto · Sydney · Tokyo · Singapore

FOR MY GIRLS

All royalties from this book will be donated to
The Prince Andrew Charitable Trust

Prentice Hall Press
15 Columbus Circle
New York, New York, 10023

Previously published in Great Britain
by Weidenfeld and Nicolson Limited.

PRENTICE HALL PRESS and colophons are registered
trademarks of Simon & Schuster Inc.

Library of Congress Cataloging-in-Publication data
on file at the Library of Congress. Available on request.

ISBN: 0-13-950882-1

Manufactured in the United States of America

First Edition

10 9 8 7 6 5 4 3 2 1

ENDPAPERS: The Solent with Osborne in the distance;
a watercolour by Prince Alfred, 24 May 1858.

PAGE 1: Frontispiece to Queen Victoria's own album of paintings.

PAGE 2: Detail from *The Marriage of Queen Victoria*
and Prince Albert, by Hayter, 1840.

CONTENTS

PREFACE

*M*y fascination with Queen Victoria, both as a monarch, but more especially as a wife and mother of a large family, is long-standing, but in March 1988, some nineteen months after my marriage to Prince Andrew, my curiosity was given new fuel by a visit to Osborne House, the home that the Queen and her consort created together on the Isle of Wight. I was immediately struck by the atmosphere of the house, and by the relatively small and intimate rooms, which were both personal and friendly. I found that I wanted to find out more about this private family home and the many days spent by Queen Victoria and her family there.

On his marriage to Queen Victoria in 1840, Prince Albert lost the freedom of his Coburg childhood and took on a new life of duty and public service. The pressures of the press and public engagements were not so great then as now, but it is still easy to sympathize with the young couple wishing to have a place away from everyday royal life. They wanted a place of their own that had not previously been a royal residence and thus would not have former associations at every turn. The Prince had always found solace in the natural world as an antidote to city life and at Osborne they found a place to escape from the pressures of London and Windsor, of court life and public scrutiny.

When I began to think of how I could discover more about what I felt must have been a magical family life on the Isle of Wight, I found that Queen Victoria's diaries and letters give a vivid and detailed description of exactly what went on there. They confirmed all my initial suppositions about how happy the couple and their children had been there. We are extremely lucky that she was such a meticulous recorder of her life and times and that her remarkable journals and much of her correspondence have been safely preserved in the Royal Archives at Windsor Castle. In the years following the

Queen Victoria, by F. X. Winterhalter, 1843. This was Albert's favourite portrait of the Queen.

Queen's death in 1901, at her specific command, the diaries were edited and considerably shortened by her youngest daughter, Princess Beatrice (after whom my own daughter was named). After the initial disappointment that they were not in their original state, I found that the diaries do still contain a huge amount of invaluable and very detailed material. There are over 110 tightly-bound manuscript volumes containing several million words. Using the excellent index to the diaries and letters which exists in the Royal Archives, it was therefore possible to put together a very clear and vivid picture of the family's life at Osborne.

Parts of this extraordinary resource have been used by researchers before, but none have taken Osborne as the central theme and used it to illustrate the close relationship between Queen Victoria and Prince Albert and their family as I have tried to do. It is exciting, therefore, to be breaking this new ground. I found that accounts of the days at Osborne reflect the development of their lives from early marriage, the raising of their children, and right through to the period of the Queen's use of the house as a place of sanctuary after Prince Albert's death. But, as my first interest is here, I have emphasized the period before his death, concentrating on the house and the years of greatest happiness.

And it seems to throw much new light onto the characters of Queen Victoria and Prince Albert. In particular I think it shows the Prince as a far more cheerful and family-orientated person than one is normally led to believe. The existing image of him has, quite correctly, emphasized his very wide interests and great efforts to help and encourage a large number of worthy causes, as well as to act as the Queen's closest adviser and, in effect, her principal private secretary. He is seen as a serious and conscientious man whose involvement even with his children was primarily motivated by feelings of duty and the greater good; and particularly with Bertie, the Prince of Wales, his attitude has usually been seen as severe and overcritical.

I therefore find it particularly interesting that from the Archives material Prince Albert comes across as a very warm, loving and even playful father who encouraged his children to do all manner of things at Osborne. Inevitably, some of these were decidedly dry and educational – though we can speculate that he may have invested even these activities with fun – such as collecting fossils and other objects for the children's museum; and he undoubtedly insisted on a high standard of manners, dealing out what the Queen referred to as his 'dear reprimands' at table. But many of his activities with his children were delightfully easy going and greatly enjoyed by all. He played with them, encouraged them to bathe in the sea (which was more avant-garde then than one would expect) and in particular built the Swiss Cottage for them. This replica of a Swiss chalet may have had an educational purpose, but it was primarily intended for fun, and became a superb retreat for the children. They tried their own cookery in the fully-equipped kitchen and Prince Albert sometimes joined in by cooking 'a German dish'.

The Prince was greatly concerned that his children should not be spoilt and wished to make them aware of how others lived; hence, they had to cultivate their own gardens next to the Swiss Cottage, each one growing flowers and vegetables, and were paid for doing various chores. It can easily be argued that they were far from normal in situation or upbringing, but Prince Albert was aware of the need to give them a broad education and tried his best to achieve this. His methods were probably in marked contrast to some of the children's aristocratic contemporaries.

It seems that Osborne was a place where the family came first. Although Queen Victoria's red despatch boxes followed her there and she diligently dealt with the official business in them, it is clear from her journal that it was the children whose existence was, after that of her beloved Albert, most important to her at Osborne. Both the Queen and Prince seemed to have spent far more time with their children than one usually associates with Victorian life. They ate together, and walked, rode, played and painted together. And the fond parents were often present at bath time in the nurseries that Prince Albert had designed close at hand. This seems an admirably far cry from the familiar Victorian pattern of the children being brought up in the nursery entirely by servants and quite separate from their parents.

The charming picture of family life at Osborne also underlines the strong love that Queen Victoria clearly had for her husband. This is vividly portrayed by her innumerable references to his activities and to her great happiness with him there. But it is also tragically shown by her utter and grinding despair following the Prince's death. It is yet another indication of the importance of Osborne to the Queen that she should seek solace there after his death at Windsor in December 1861. Thereafter she always spent her wedding anniversary at Osborne and family Christmas was moved there from Windsor.

I felt the happy nature of the house was also emphasized by its use for the honeymoons of both the Prince of Wales and Princess Helena; and there are the fascinating accounts of two of her daughter's weddings at Osborne, those of Princess Alice in 1862 and Princess Beatrice in 1885. It is difficult to think of two more dissimilar occasions. Alice's was, in the Queen's words, 'more like a funeral than a wedding' because it came so soon after Prince Albert's death; while Beatrice's was a full-blown royal wedding, not least because she and her accommodating husband had agreed to Queen Victoria's condition of marriage: that the couple should live with the Queen so that Beatrice could continue to support her.

It is this selfishness after Prince Albert's death that is one aspect of the Queen's character that this study has brought home to me. Our view of her at Osborne is of a caring and loving mother. After her tragic loss Victoria was clearly so devastated that far from giving her children the support they so needed, they had to try to help her. Subsequently, she expected them to put their own lives and happiness second to hers. Queen Victoria expected a daughter always to be on hand to act as her companion and private secretary.

The depth of the Queen's depression after Prince Albert's death would surely nowadays be considered in terms of a nervous breakdown and treated as such. But from her writings it seems that she was left alone with her grief and committed her gloom to her diary and letters: her unique position would have made any outside help impossible to give unless she herself solicited it. So, like a wounded animal creeping away to its lair, the Queen made Osborne with all its Albertian associations her sanctuary.

Although Osborne was a haven from public life, it inevitably acted as a backdrop for official visits, and thus political events. Napoleon III and his wife, the Empress Eugénie (after whom Princess Beatrice named her daughter and hence our Eugenie), were invited there in 1857. We also have the Queen's view of Britain's future enemy in World War I, Kaiser William II of Germany. As Queen Victoria's eldest grandson, he made his first family visit to Osborne aged two and a half, in August 1861. Even then it seems that his violence made his four-year-old aunt, Princess Beatrice, afraid of him. This close family relationship of Queen Victoria with the German and other European royal families of the day reminds one how closely Britain was involved with Europe at that time; and it is perhaps surprising how little obviously Germanic influence was absorbed into the family's life from Prince Albert's own background.

As I read more about the Queen and Prince and their life at Osborne, some coincidental but appealing facts emerged. Queen Victoria herself was meticulous about remembering significant dates and noting when they coincided; one of her least favourite was 14 December, anniversary of the death of her beloved Albert and of her second daughter Princess Alice (Prince Philip's great-grandmother). I very soon found that our wedding day, 23 July, coincided with the wedding at Osborne of Princess Beatrice to Prince Henry of Battenberg; moreover, my bouquet contained myrtle from Osborne just as Beatrice's had, and our page boys wore sailor suits copied from F. X. Winterhalter's portrait of 1846 of the Prince of Wales. Other coincidences of date included Queen Victoria proposing to Prince Albert on 15 October, my birthday. These strange connections merely served to increase my fascination with the royal couple, and with Osborne House itself.

As Prince Andrew and I planned, and finally saw the completion of, our own new home at Sunninghill in Berkshire, I felt increasingly close to Queen Victoria and understood her own and Prince Albert's desire to create a special private place in which to share their lives together and to bring up their children away from the pressures of public life. My own pleasure in seeing Andrew's enthusiasm for the development of the plans – weekends spent standing in a muddy field trying to imagine the position of rooms – and his active interest in daily progress must have been closely akin to Queen Victoria's shared joy with Prince Albert. My abiding impression on completion of this book is of a truly great and all-consuming love which, because of the identity of the couple, has left its mark indelibly on history.

Part of Osborne House is currently open to the public from May to October each year. This contains the private apartments where Queen Victoria and her family lived; and at her specific request it has been left more or less as it was when she used it. And she in turn had left much of it just as it had been when dear Albert was still alive. I would warmly recommend people to visit it, to experience the atmosphere and to truly appreciate this extraordinary memorial to Queen Victoria and Prince Albert's marriage that I feel has been sadly neglected.

ACKNOWLEDGEMENTS

I am particularly grateful to Her Majesty The Queen for having allowed me full access to the Royal Archives at Windsor Castle. All material from the Archives is published by gracious permission of Her Majesty.

I should also like to express my very special and heartfelt thanks to my friend Benita Stoney for her painstaking and meticulous research. Our shared enthusiasm for the subject was what made the whole project possible, and her continual sense of humour eased the long hours. It is more to her credit than mine that the book has been completed.

We received the unfailing help of the staff in the Royal Archives and Royal Library, in particular from Sheila de Bellaigue, Pamela Clark, Frances Dimond, Jane Roberts, Bridget Wright and Stephen Patterson. Benita's research also owes much to the kind assistance of Lucy Cadogan, Paula Iley, Nicola Kennedy, John Paton, Mr E. Sibbick and Robert Stoney.

It simply would not be correct to go a line further without acknowledging the strength and deep continual support of Oliver Everett. Without him I could not have taken on such a project and I am so very grateful for his endless hours of help and advice. Oliver is and was always there for questions and historical facts. Benita stayed with Oliver and Theffania Everett, and I know she owes her greatest debt, and mine, to them both.

I am also grateful to Lord Mishcon and Lord Weidenfeld for their personal interest and support with the initiation and fulfilment of this project; and to Michael Dover and Alice Millington-Drake for their detailed work on the production of the book.

Last, but not least, to my tolerant secretary Jane Ambler – a really special thank you.

THE DESCENDANTS OF
QUEEN VICTORIA

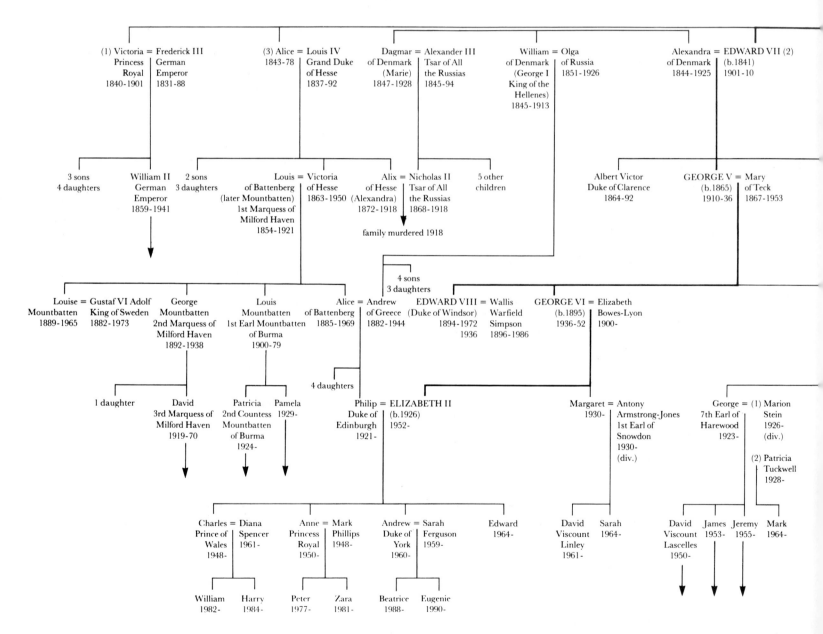

(1) Victoria = **Frederick III**
Princess | German
Royal | Emperor
1840-1901 | 1831-88

(3) Alice = **Louis IV**
1843-78 | Grand Duke
of Hesse
1837-92

Dagmar = **Alexander III**
of Denmark | Tsar of All
(Marie) | the Russias
1847-1928 | 1845-94

William = **Olga**
of Denmark | of Russia
(George I | 1851-1926
King of the
Hellenes)
1845-1913

Alexandra = **EDWARD VII (2)**
of Denmark | (b.1841)
1844-1925 | 1901-10

3 sons
4 daughters

William II
German
Emperor
1859-1941

2 sons
3 daughters

Louis = **Victoria**
of Battenberg | of Hesse
(later Mountbatten) | 1863-1950
1st Marquess of
Milford Haven
1854-1921

Alix = **Nicholas II**
of Hesse | Tsar of All
(Alexandra) | the Russias
1872-1918 | 1868-1918

family murdered 1918

5 other
children

Albert Victor
Duke of Clarence
1864-92

GEORGE V = **Mary**
(b.1865) | of Teck
1910-36 | 1867-1953

4 sons
3 daughters

Louise = **Gustaf VI Adolf**
Mountbatten | King of Sweden
1889-1965 | 1882-1973

George
Mountbatten
2nd Marquess of
Milford Haven
1892-1938

Louis
Mountbatten
1st Earl Mountbatten
of Burma
1900-79

Alice = **Andrew**
of Battenberg | of Greece
1885-1969 | 1882-1944

EDWARD VIII = **Wallis**
(Duke of Windsor) | Warfield
1894-1972 | Simpson
1936 | 1896-1986

GEORGE VI = **Elizabeth**
(b.1895) | Bowes-Lyon
1936-52 | 1900-

Margaret = **Antony**
1930- | Armstrong-Jones
1st Earl of
Snowdon
1930-
(div.)

George = **(1) Marion**
7th Earl of | Stein
Harewood | 1926-
1923- | (div.)

(2) Patricia
Tuckwell
1928-

1 daughter

David
3rd Marquess of
Milford Haven
1919-70

Patricia
2nd Countess
Mountbatten
of Burma
1924-

Pamela
1929-

4 daughters

Philip = **ELIZABETH II**
Duke of | (b.1926)
Edinburgh | 1952-
1921-

David
Viscount
Linley
1961-

Sarah
1964-

David
Viscount
Lascelles
1950-

James
1953-

Jeremy
1955-

Mark
1964-

Charles = **Diana**
Prince of | Spencer
Wales | 1961-
1948-

Anne = **Mark**
Princess | Phillips
Royal | 1948-
1950-

Andrew = **Sarah**
Duke of | Ferguson
York | 1959-
1960-

Edward
1964-

William
1982-

Harry
1984-

Peter
1977-

Zara
1981-

Beatrice
1988-

Eugenie
1990-

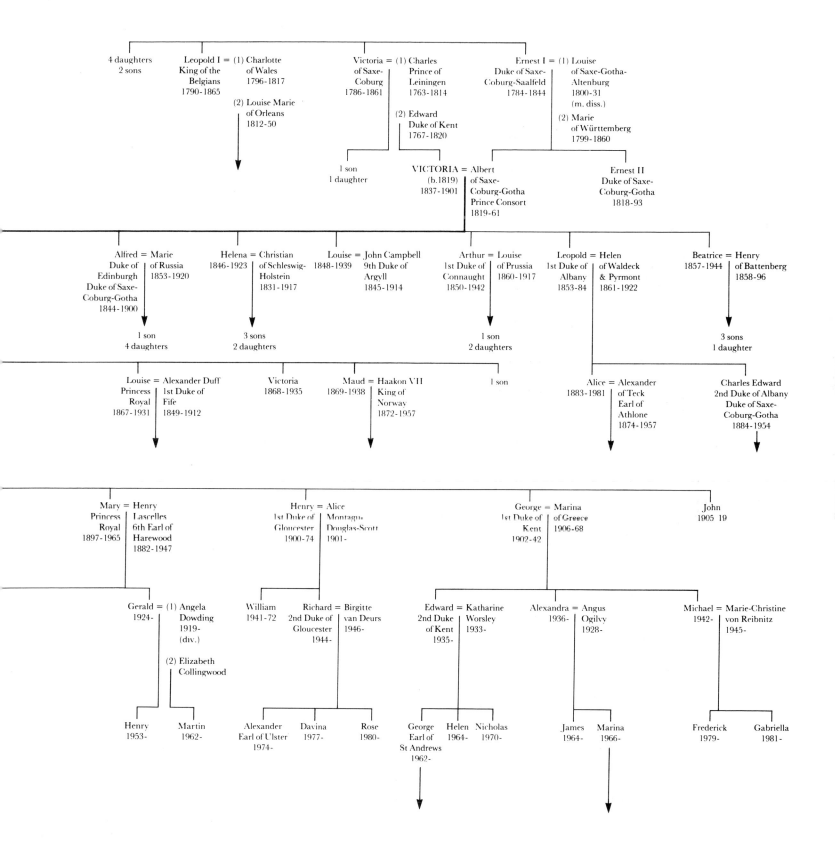

4 daughters
2 sons

Leopold I = (1) Charlotte
King of the | of Wales
Belgians | 1796-1817
1790-1865

(2) Louise Marie
of Orleans
1812-50

Victoria = (1) Charles
of Saxe- | Prince of
Coburg | Leiningen
1786-1861 | 1763-1814

(2) Edward
Duke of Kent
1767-1820

Ernest I = (1) Louise
Duke of Saxe- | of Saxe-Gotha-
Coburg-Saalfeld | Altenburg
1784-1844 | 1800-31
(m. diss.)

(2) Marie
of Württemberg
1799-1860

1 son
1 daughter

VICTORIA = Albert
(b.1819) | of Saxe-
1837-1901 | Coburg-Gotha
| Prince Consort
| 1819-61

Ernest II
Duke of Saxe-
Coburg-Gotha
1818-93

Alfred = Marie
Duke of | of Russia
Edinburgh | 1853-1920
Duke of Saxe-
Coburg-Gotha
1844-1900

Helena = Christian
1846-1923 | of Schleswig-
| Holstein
| 1831-1917

Louise = John Campbell
1848-1939 | 9th Duke of
| Argyll
| 1845-1914

Arthur = Louise
1st Duke of | of Prussia
Connaught | 1860-1917
1850-1942

Leopold = Helen
1st Duke of | of Waldeck
Albany | & Pyrmont
1853-84 | 1861-1922

Beatrice = Henry
1857-1944 | of Battenberg
| 1858-96

1 son
4 daughters

3 sons
2 daughters

1 son
2 daughters

3 sons
1 daughter

Louise = Alexander Duff
Princess | 1st Duke of
Royal | Fife
1867-1931 | 1849-1912

Victoria
1868-1935

Maud = Haakon VII
1869-1938 | King of
| Norway
| 1872-1957

1 son

Alice = Alexander
1883-1981 | of Teck
| Earl of
| Athlone
| 1874-1957

Charles Edward
2nd Duke of Albany
Duke of Saxe-
Coburg-Gotha
1884-1954

Mary = Henry
Princess | Lascelles
Royal | 6th Earl of
1897-1965 | Harewood
| 1882-1947

Henry = Alice
1st Duke of | Montagu-
Gloucester | Douglas-Scott
1900-74 | 1901-

George = Marina
1st Duke of | of Greece
Kent | 1906-68
1902-42

John
1905 19

Gerald = (1) Angela
1924- | Dowding
| 1919-
| (div.)

(2) Elizabeth
Collingwood

William
1941-72

Richard = Birgitte
2nd Duke of | van Deurs
Gloucester | 1946-
1944-

Edward = Katharine
2nd Duke | Worsley
of Kent | 1933-
1935-

Alexandra = Angus
1936- | Ogilvy
| 1928-

Michael = Marie-Christine
1942- | von Reibnitz
| 1945-

Henry
1953-

Martin
1962-

Alexander
Earl of Ulster
1974-

Davina
1977-

Rose
1980-

George
Earl of
St Andrews
1962-

Helen
1964-

Nicholas
1970-

James
1964-

Marina
1966-

Frederick
1979-

Gabriella
1981-

CHAPTER ONE

THE FIRST YEARS
OF MARRIAGE

*I*t was with some emotion that I beheld Albert – who is *beautiful*.'[1] These were the private thoughts of the twenty-year-old Queen of England as she stood at the top of the staircase at Windsor Castle in October 1839 to receive the prince who had come for her inspection. She had met him once before, when they were both sixteen, and though she had liked him then, she was only seeing him now because she must.

He for his part, had come with every intention of putting an end to whatever nebulous agreement there was between them – an agreement, it should be said, that existed largely in the heads of the Queen's two Coburg uncles, one of whom happened to be the young man's father. It was a difficult moment for two people who were not much more than puppets dancing on the end of dynastic strings.

Princess Victoria had been born in 1819, shortly before the death of her father the Duke of Kent, heiress to a throne that had become a byword for all that was expensive, scandalous and unpopular. She was brought up by her mother, the Duchess of Kent, and would later remember her childhood as a period sheltered and simple to the point of melancholy isolation. It was darkened by a web of scheming and intrigue, principally of her mother's weaving, which forced unnatural restraints on Victoria's frank and spontaneous nature. Many years later, as Queen, Victoria would remember how she had had no outlet for her 'very violent feelings of affection – had no brothers or sisters to live with – never had a father – from my unfortunate circumstances was not on a comfortable or at all intimate or confidential footing with my mother . . . and did not know what a happy domestic life was.'[2]

Her cousin Albert, born a few months after Victoria in the minor German principality of Coburg, the second son of the Duchess of Kent's brother, Duke Ernest of Saxe-Coburg-Saalfeld, had a happier, though not cloudless, childhood. Like Victoria, he grew up with only one parent, for when he was five, his

Miniature of Prince Albert, by William Ross, painted at the time of the Prince's engagement.

pretty, vivacious mother left Coburg, and her two sons, for ever, having made the mistake of believing that her husband would tolerate in her the morals which he practised himself, and that she too could stray from the straight and narrow path of marital fidelity. Divorce followed. Albert and his older brother Ernest were lucky in that the bond between them was close and loving, in spite of their very different characters, and that they were provided with a stern, but humane and enlightened tutor who drew out the best of their talents. They largely grew up in the rural surroundings of the Rosenau, the country residence of the Dukes of Coburg, set among wooded hills and valleys four miles out of the city. The young Albert always regarded the Rosenau as his real home, and was happiest there. His education was given a final polish by the University of Bonn, and the conventional Grand Tour in Italy.

It was Duke Ernest's cherished ambition that Albert, who otherwise had only the meagre prospects of any younger son before him, should carry off the richest prize in Europe, his English cousin. Duke Ernest had a useful ally in his brother, Leopold, King of the Belgians, who Princess Victoria knew well, trusted and regarded as a second father.

Leopold engineered a cousinly visit which the two brothers paid to England in 1836. Princess Victoria was diverted enough to send Uncle Leopold some primly dutiful observations on her cousin: 'Allow me then, my dearest Uncle, to tell you how delighted I am with him, and how much I like him in every way. He possesses every quality that could be desired to render me perfectly happy. He is so sensible, so kind, and so good, and so amiable too. He has, besides, the most pleasing and delightful exterior and appearance you can possibly see.'[3] But she did not fall in love, nor commit herself, and there the matter rested. Prince Albert of Saxe-Coburg-Gotha was just one of several princely possibilities on Victoria's marital horizon.

The Princess-in-waiting became Queen, sipped at the honeyed wells of independence and power, and acquired a taste for them. As she stood at the top of the staircase, she dreaded the thought of marrying at all: she had not wished to see Albert (the whole subject was an odious one); she was nervous about the visit; she did not wish to marry for two or three years at least; and while she had heard very good reports of her cousin, and knew that she could like him 'as a *friend*, and as a *cousin*, and as a *brother*', she was not sure that she could like him enough for a husband. As she herself pointed out, 'one can never answer beforehand for *feelings* and I may not have the *feeling* for him which is requisite to ensure happiness.'[4]

But as she looked down at the blue eyes and light brown hair, the pretty mouth furnished with 'delicate moustachios and slight, but very slight whiskers',[5] the broad shoulders and fine waist, of the young man who ascended the staircase towards her, reluctance gave way to surprise and dawning pleasure. He was so grown and changed, so 'embellished' since their last meeting, that her feelings began to catch up with her in a way that she had not anticipated.

During the course of the next few days, Victoria discovered anew how 'passionately fond' of music he was; and that it was 'quite a pleasure' to watch her graceful cousin dancing and riding, while an evening in his company could be delightful. With a beating heart she inscribed his personal beauties in her journal; her German cousin was, 'in short, very fascinating'. After only five

Miniature of Queen Victoria, by William Ross, 1838.

Prince Albert, by the Queen, 1839, a pencil copy of a portrait by William Ross, and one of the very few sketches which Victoria attempted of him (detail).

OPPOSITE: Queen Victoria's mother, the Duchess of Kent, by Winterhalter, 1846. The Duchess was later to give the painting as a birthday present to the Queen.

Programme for a musical evening, which took place at Windsor Castle, two days after the Queen had proposed to Albert. He has covered the blank sheet with sketches and caricatures, among them the long nose of a greyhound. The Queen has noted in the corner, 'Dearest Albert drew them in the Drawing Room on Oct. 17th 1839.'

Letter written in German from the Queen to Prince Albert during their engagement.

days in his company she had made her decision. On 15 October 1839 Albert was summoned to the Blue Closet, and after a few moments Queen Victoria proposed to him – as so often, the Queen had to undertake tasks usually in the domain of the man – and was accepted.

They were married in the Chapel Royal at St James's Palace on 10 February 1840. The Queen wore the sapphire brooch which had been Albert's wedding present, and the creamy white dresses of the bride and her bridesmaids contrasted dramatically with the gorgeous colours and jewels of the jostling peers around them. Cynics tittered when Albert promised to endow her with all his worldly goods, but kinder eyes observed the look of great happiness in her face, and 'her look of confidence and comfort at the Prince as they walked away as man and wife.'[6]

They spent their two-day honeymoon at Windsor. Albert had suggested it might be longer, and had earned himself a queenly rebuke:

You forget, my dearest Love, that *I* am the *Sovereign*, and that business can stop and wait for *nothing*. Parliament is sitting, and something occurs *almost every day*, for which I may be required, and it is *quite impossible* for me to be absent from London; therefore two or three days is already a *long time* to be absent. I am never easy a moment, if I am not on the spot, and see and hear what is going on.[7]

It is a revealing letter; this is the maiden Queen speaking, the girl who enjoyed being at the centre of things, who danced until three in the morning and declared that such 'dissipation' did her good; vicarious stimulation that compensated for her own, hitherto arid emotional life. It was written before she had learnt to defer to her husband, before he had left his indelible imprint on her character, before she had moulded herself around him, like ivy round an oak. Many years later she was to say of herself that she had a clinging nature.

Marriage changed the Queen. At last she had a companion with whom she no longer had to guard her tongue; within the confines of marriage she found a

Queen Victoria reading, by William Ross, 1841. The Queen initially excluded Albert from affairs of state and worked alone; later, she came to rely on him completely.

A more formal miniature of Prince Albert, by William Ross, 1840.

new freedom. While Victoria's galloping pen breathlessly charted every new experience, so that we are in no doubt as to her deep and incredulous joy, Albert has left no like testimonials. He was rarely inclined to commit his soul to paper; it is visible in the affection he inspired in those who were close to him, even in the Queen's unquestioning worship, and in the tangible monuments he left: the institutions he founded and fostered, and the houses he built.

The new husband faced a difficult future, virtually alone in a foreign country, with no companions from his old life except a few personal servants. He took second place to his wife in everything save the precedence accorded him by her own heart; and even in that tempestuous organ the hot-tempered Queen could overrule the thoughtful wife. Furthermore, the rooms that he lived in, the paintings on the walls, the furniture, everything belonged to the monarch. The normal difficulties of early married life – the inevitable storms and power struggles as two very different characters came to know one another – were compounded by the reversal of normal roles. The Queen expressed it in her usual succinct way: 'Albert is in my house and not I in his.'[8]

Prince Albert and his eldest child, Victoria, the Princess Royal, by Edwin Landseer, c.1841; she was always known to her family as Vicky.

Queen Victoria with her two eldest children, by Landseer, 1842. Albert Edward, Prince of Wales, known as Bertie, arrived before Vicky's first birthday. The Queen had hoped for a few years' freedom before she began to have children.

The palaces were run according to obsolete traditions and half-forgotten customs – fires, for instance, were laid by one department, but lit by another; one department cleaned the outside of the windows, another the inside. After a year or two the Prince, an efficient bureaucrat, had swept away some of the finer lunacies of palace life (and earned no thanks from those who lost their perquisites), but still the public departments remained. The Department of Woods and Forests, ancestor of the modern Department of the Environment, was Albert's particular irritation, and at every turn hampered his ideas for improving the palaces, and for making them more comfortable for himself, his wife and the children. By August 1844, four years and six months after they were married, Victoria and Albert already had two sons and two daughters.

Added to the frustrations of being 'only the husband, not the master in the house', was Albert's new way of life. It did not suit him. During the first few years of Victoria and Albert's marriage the Court journeyed back and forth between Buckingham Palace and Windsor Castle. Life in these splendid residences was inconvenient, and even hazardous. Buckingham Palace, on which the Queen's uncle, George IV, had spent half a million pounds of public money – a sum which still smarted in the public memory twenty years later – had no better sanitation than the neighbouring slums, haunted by the lurking spectres of cholera and typhoid, and fumes from the charcoal burning stoves in the palace kitchens escaped into the attic nurseries, hardly suitable accommodation for the burgeoning royal brood.

Some of the disadvantages of Buckingham Palace were inescapable afflictions of city life. In winter, a coal fire burned in the grate of every Londoner who could afford it; a dark red, fiery sun smouldered through heavy grey smog, and a fall of snow would soon be covered in soot; palace furniture was speckled with black particles in a matter of hours and shining silver quickly tarnished. It was impossible for the Queen's maids to leave any article of clothing lying about, and even in cupboards everything became dirty.

Inside the tall grey battlements of Windsor Castle, free from the worst of the London smogs, there was more room for children, Household and servants; but at that time the Castle had no private gardens; there was nowhere for the royal couple to take their daily walk in private, and here Victoria and Albert felt more than ever that they were 'slaves to the public'. Besides, the place reminded Victoria uncomfortably of her childhood in the bilious atmosphere of her mother's quarrels with the old royal family: 'always on pins and needles, with the whole family hardly on speaking terms. I (a mere child) between two fires – trying to be civil and scolded at home! Oh! it was dreadful, and that has given me a horror of Windsor, which I can't get over.'[9]

Albert was at heart a countryman, and his spirits always suffered from staying in London too long. The kind of 'dissipation' which invigorated the Queen left Albert looking pale and wan. For a wholesome change from London or Windsor they would spend a week or two in the elegant tranquillity of Claremont, eighteen miles from Windsor, which belonged to King Leopold. Here the Prince was 'as happy and cheerful' as he looked 'sleepy and dull' in London; sagacious Lady Lyttelton, the most perceptive of the Queen's ladies-in-waiting, realized that 'the poor man likes nothing but *das land leben*', or country life; and correctly predicted that the Queen was 'so complying towards him that he may lead her to like it too at last'.[10] However, whereas Albert

obtained a deep solace from the natural world, an antidote to the artificiality of city life, the Queen grew to like it because he did, and because it provided her with an escape from the glare of publicity, as she wrote regretfully after one visit to Claremont: 'God knows how willingly I would always live with my beloved Albert and our children in the quiet and retirement of private life, and not be the constant object of observation, and of newspaper articles.'[11]

In those days, great importance was given to clean, pure air. Sea air, in particular, was felt to have healthy, bracing virtues. If the royal couple felt the need for such a tonic, it was abundantly available to them at Brighton Pavilion, which Victoria's uncle had built when Prince Regent. However, this seaside pleasure palace held no charms for the young couple. The Queen condemned

Windsor Castle in Modern Times, by Landseer, *c.*1842. Albert's position, as consort of a reigning Queen, was not easy; the purchase and rebuilding of Osborne House did much to resolve it.

The promenade of the royal family in the Palace gardens, 1842–44. Life in London was even more restricted than at Windsor Castle; a promenade around the sooty shrubberies of Buckingham Palace Gardens was a poor substitute for life in the country.

the Prince Regent's outmoded extravaganza as 'a strange, odd, Chinese looking thing'. It was completely lacking in privacy and no longer any use as a marine residence. Since the Prince Regent's day the suburbs of the town had come crowding round the cupolas and minarets of the Pavilion, just like the citizens of the town who mobbed the Queen on her rare visits, and now only a glimpse of the sea was visible from the Queen's sitting room. Besides, the extravagant, feverish interiors where dragons writhed along fenders and pelmets, and the King's mistresses stared insolently down from the murals round the dining room, were not apartments in which the young Queen, as much bourgeoise as sovereign, felt comfortable.

Castle, palace, pavilion or house – all had one drawback in common: they did not belong to the Queen personally and therefore in none were she and Albert free to do as they chose. On 19 October 1843, during their usual morning walk, they discussed buying a place of their own, 'which would be so nice', said the Queen wistfully, adding that 'perhaps Norris Castle might be something to think of'.[12] She had stayed there as a child when the Duchess of Kent took her to the Isle of Wight for the summer in 1831 and 1833. Victoria's dogs had swum in the sea, and the Princess had cantered her pony into the neighbouring property of Osborne, which she had noticed in passing was such a pretty lodge. After she came to the throne, Norris Castle had been offered to her for £15,000, but she turned it down, a decision which, years later, she came to regret.[13] But in 1839 she had not yet married Albert and learnt his country ways, and was still, perhaps, too close to her childhood, too close to memories of being put out on the landing with her hands tied behind her back when she was naughty.[14]

Victoria and Albert consulted the Prime Minister, Sir Robert Peel, and thoughts of Norris were soon superseded by his suggestion that they look into the possibilities of the Osborne Estate, which he had heard was up for sale. On paper, Osborne seemed to supply everything that they were looking for, and before Christmas they were already talking of buying it. Albert was not, however, going to spend the asking price of £28,000, which would come out of the Queen's personal fortune, on a place which did not completely suit them. He proposed that they should rent the house for an experimental year while they made up their minds; this arrangement, he insisted, 'conditional upon my liking the place after personal inspection'.[15] On 18 March 1844, he got up at daybreak to go down to view Osborne, returning to the Queen that evening, 'much pleased', she wrote that day, 'with Osborne, its size, its privacy, etc., but says that to render the house completely comfortable it will have to be added to.' Osborne was taken for one year at a rent of £1,000 from 1 May 1844.

The following October, in continual violent showers of rain, Queen Victoria and Prince Albert sailed across the Solent to the Isle of Wight and drove up to Osborne House on the outskirts of East Cowes. As they turned into the grounds, which the Queen observed to be 'delightfully private', the sun came out and lit up a large, three-storey, eighteenth-century house, with a plain symmetrical façade and an elegant fanlight over the front door. Around it stood tall trees; and beyond the ground sloped away down towards the sea, so that as Victoria and Albert alighted from their carriage they could see far across the waters of the Solent, busy with steamships and sails, to the distant anchorage of Spithead, and the gentle curves of the downs beyond.

Vicky, by Prince Albert, *c*.1841. The Prince adored his eldest daughter.

Old Osborne House, by C. R. Stanley, 1844. Albert planned a few modest alterations; later, only the front door remained, set into the garden wall.

Bertie and Vicky, by
Prince Albert, c.1842. It
was Albert, not the Queen,
who directed the running
of the nurseries.

Victoria and Albert stayed at Osborne for six days to make up their minds.
From the very first moment the Queen was delighted, and then, as the
possibilities of the place began to open up, enchanted. The house was '*so
complete and snug*', said the Queen; it had everything, from library and wine
cellar to nursery, icehouse, and piggeries, to make it 'a comfortable and very
commodious residence for any Gentleman and family'.[16] The rooms seemed
small after Buckingham Palace and Windsor Castle; nevertheless royalty
declared itself to be very comfortably lodged, decided that the house was light,
cheerful, dry and warm, and that with 'some few alterations and additions for
the children it might be made an excellent home'.[17]

They ventured further afield, full of admiration for the island scenery,
revelling in their 'quite unmolested' exploration of the woods and fields of
Osborne and the adjoining farm of Barton which formed part of the property;
even walking along the high road they 'hardly met a soul'. The estate ran down
to the sea, and on the shore Victoria and Albert walked along firm sand, the
Queen exclaiming over the 'quantities of pretty shells', Albert's practical eye
noticing the excellent bathing places. If they did decide to buy Osborne, it
would become their marine residence, so they undertook experimental trips in
various forms of waterborne transport, rowing about in their barge, trying out
different steamers, and going out to the Needles at the western end of the island.
It was during one of these excursions that another enchanting prospect dawned

on the Queen: they would be able to embark and disembark from their own grounds. Albert pointed out that the 'healthful enjoyment' of being out at sea daily would bring the royal family into close contact with 'that glorious profession', the Navy. In every way Osborne fulfilled the careful list of 'prudent and necessary' requirements which he had drawn up: it was in a beautiful – and healthy – position; would give its inhabitants absolute privacy; and yet the journey to London and the heart of affairs only took four hours on the new railways. Moreover, said the businesslike Prince, who had already done much to improve his wife's financial affairs in the four years they had been married, Osborne could probably be purchased 'at not too great a sacrifice of money'. Albert continued, speaking as much for himself as his wife:

The Queen has long wished to have a property of her own, in which she can do what she likes, is responsible to nobody, uncontrolled by the public, unimpeded by Government Commissioners and Household Officers, which she could leave to her children. This wish is so reasonable and the accomplishment of it will in my opinion be such a source of amusement, comfort, and satisfaction to her, myself, and our family, that I think it ought to be fulfilled.[18]

After their October stay, negotiations to purchase began in earnest. It was a complicated transaction, made more so by the personality of the vendor, Lady Isabella Blachford. Osborne itself, the house and some 342 acres, belonged entirely to her, whilst Barton Farm, another 500 acres – without which Albert would not consider buying Osborne – she held on a long lease from Winchester College. Albert wished to own Barton outright, or freehold, so not only did he have to negotiate with Lady Isabella for her interest in the current lease, but also with the Warden and Scholars of Winchester, who could not sell church property without an Act of Parliament. Obtaining the Act was a

Part of the memorandum, written at Osborne on Trafalgar Day, in which Albert set out his reasons for purchasing the property which became Her Majesty's marine residence. That afternoon he and the Queen, passing through Gosport, went over HMS *Victory*.

Princess Alice, the third
child, with Albert's
favourite greyhound, Eos,
by Landseer, 1844.

straightforward affair, however, compared to dealing with Lady Isabella. She
bargained hard, changed her mind, quarrelled with her own solicitors,
protested rather too vehemently that she was not taking advantage, and drove
Albert's hard-pressed Private Secretary George Anson to declare that she was
'a tiresome person to have anything to do with, and the sooner she was paid and
done with the better'.[19] Sir Robert Peel found her behaviour 'quite unaccoun-
table', and even the Queen complained of her 'extreme obstinacy in trying to
squeeze everything out of us she can'.[20] There are two sides to every story, and
Lady Isabella could be said to have had some cause for complaint. On 21
March 1845 she finally accepted £26,000, an offer that was some £5,500 less
than the price she had asked at the outset. Disagreements over the valuation of
furniture, fixtures, and crops dragged on for the rest of the year, and it was
November before Lady Isabella was finally 'paid and done with'.

To round off the property of Osborne and Barton, Victoria and Albert
bought various neighbouring farms. One or two, such as Alverstone and
Woodhouse, had almost as much land as Osborne, others just a few acres; by the
end of December 1847 they had spent a total of £67,000 on an estate of 1,727
acres. A sinking fund of £18,600 was put aside to pay Winchester for the
freehold of Barton when the existing lease ran out in November 1862. Even if
the suburbs of another Brighton were to sprout up at their very gates, inside
their 'immense' possessions (the Queen's expression) Victoria and Albert would
now always be assured of the strictest privacy.

From the moment Lady Isabella finally accepted the offer, the Queen
regarded Osborne as '*our own* property which is a *great* satisfaction', and happily
dashed off a letter to Uncle Leopold with the news, which she was sure he would
be glad to hear: 'It sounds so snug and nice to have a place of *one's own* and quiet

Alice, Bertie and Vicky, by the Queen, March 1845 (*left*). A few months later she sketched a self portrait, 19 May 1845 (*above*).

and retired, and free from all Woods and Forests and other charming departments who really are the plague of one's life.'[21]

The Queen's Household were not nearly so overjoyed, indeed were frankly dismayed that the royal couple 'would rather prefer any cottage-looking thing to a castle, for a change'; Sir James Clarke, Physician in Ordinary to the Queen felt that the sea air on the Isle of Wight was not bracing enough to do the children any good; while to George Anson the price seemed 'very dear', particularly since they had 'everything to do'.[22]

It was just this aspect of Osborne which had the greatest appeal for Albert. For here was an energetic man of twenty-six whose innovative intelligence was hardly satisfied by his role in life as husband of the Queen. He had not yet carved out his position in English life, and hitherto, living in houses that did not belong to him, he had not even been master at home; now, with the purchase of Osborne, he could at least be that. In the badly-farmed, exhausted fields, neglected woods and dilapidated farm buildings, and a house that already he had admitted was too small, Albert saw a blank canvas which allowed him the scope of his own devising, a realm of escape where he could command at his pleasure, experiment, improve, adorn, ordain; create a place in which his wife and family could thrive and flourish.

Alfred, or Affie as he was known, the fourth child, aged fifteen months, drawn by the Queen in November 1845.

CHAPTER TWO

THE CREATION
OF OSBORNE

he house as it is', Albert wrote on the last morning of their stay at Osborne in October 1844, 'requires no altera- tion, only the addition of a few rooms to make it a very suitable and comfortable residence for the Queen and the children and part of the suite. This addition can easily be made and if done in a plain, unassuming style conformable to the rest of the house ought not to cost a great deal.'[1] The small-scale alterations and minor repairs which he envisaged, to make Osborne more comfort- able, required the services of a builder. Albert found just the man in the person of Thomas Cubitt. One of the most eminent builders in London, Cubitt had originally trained as a carpenter, and as a ship's carpenter went to India; on his return to London he set up in business, and for thirty-five years had run a large-scale enterprise as a speculative builder. Rows of his houses could be seen all round London from Highbury to Pimlico; and he was re- sponsible for many of the smart new squares in Belgravia, just across the road from the gardens of Buckingham Palace. George Anson lived in a house of Cubitt's building in Eaton Place, and while there is no evidence that it was he who recommended Cubitt, this is the most likely link between the entrepren- eur and the Prince.

Cubitt surveyed the house and recommended that it would be better to build anew than to repair; although an opinion that coincided with his own best interests, it confirmed a suspicion which had already been voiced by a more impartial observer, the Prime Minister. Cubitt went to Osborne when the royal couple were next there, in the spring of 1845, and went over the house twice with the Prince, discussing 'a few alterations'.[2] Albert was bursting with plans; he stayed out of doors long after the Queen, 'full of altera- tions and improvements he wants to make, and so happy'.[3]

Within a few days of his return to London Albert inspected Cubitt's workshops. He saw a large, efficient organization, which could be relied upon

Detail from a watercolour by W. L. Leitch of Osborne House, 1850. This was the heart of the house, the Pavilion, where Victoria and Albert had their private apartments.

to keep to its estimates. It was an important consideration for within living memory members of the royal family had burnt their fingers badly with architects who went grossly over budget. An economical grandeur came to be the hallmark of Osborne.

On 3 April 1845 the builder was authorized to go ahead. The Queen's solicitors, in the thick of the legalities of the purchase and increasingly acrimonious correspondence with Lady Isabella, shook their heads and warned of the risks in case there were difficulties over the title, and Lady Isabella's agents arriving at Osborne to value her furniture were dismayed to find that

View from the window at Osborne, by the Queen, 1850. She never tired of this wide panorama, which she once said reminded Albert of the Bay of Naples.

Cubitt's men had already moved much of it out of the way in order to start work on the house.

Albert's guiding hand is visible in the very first item on Cubitt's list of the work done to make the eighteenth-century house more comfortable for the Queen and her Court. Although it was already well fitted with water closets, a new one was installed in the principal bedroom. Further comforts took the form of new marble chimneypieces and new stoves in the Queen's and the Prince's dressing rooms. Practical considerations of safety affixed guard bars to windows, presumably those of the nursery to stop the royal children falling out. Eight rooms were freshly papered. Wallpaper was still something of a rarity and in the homes of even Her Majesty's better-off subjects was usually reserved for a single special room.

While the workmen were improving the old house, Albert was making plans for the new with Cubitt. The Prince visited houses built by Cubitt at Albert Gate and one belonging to Lord Clare in Lowndes Square. That Albert liked what he saw of Cubitt's work on this expedition is apparent in Cubitt's

Old Osborne House, by C. R. Stanley, 1844. The Pavilion was built to the right of the house where the trees stand, and the rough ground in front was transformed into terraces and smooth lawns.

specification for the new house at Osborne, which was to be built 'with the best materials in a workmanlike manner and not inferior to the house belonging to Mr Anson in Eaton Place or Lord Clare's house in Lowndes Square.'[4]

In 1845 Victoria and Albert paid seven separate visits to their new property. The Queen's journal filled up with accounts of the island's delights. She sniffed the heavy, sweet smell of the yellow gorse which blazed along the roadsides, sipped cowslip tea after her constitutional, and with Albert, on their hill ponies, explored the wild and pretty places of their 'dear and lovely little domaine'. Her enjoyment of the island was enriched by her husband's pleasure: 'It does one's heart good', she wrote, 'to see how my beloved Albert enjoys it all, and is so full of all the plans and improvements he means to carry out. He is hardly to be kept at home a moment.'[5] On 15 May 1845 they 'walked about the house to take a last look at it *as it is now*, for we shall never see it so again. The new house will be begun tomorrow and the best trees in the place, including a fine old oak, which are near the present house, will have, alas! to be cut down.'[6]

Regret was soon overtaken by excitement when they returned the

Thomas Cubitt's watercolour of his plan for Osborne, 1845. It differs in architectural detail from the house that was actually built, and it is probable that these refinements were Albert's.

following month; certainly the digging of foundations, to the north of the old house on the seaward side, made a 'great mess' in front of the house, but the island was like a garden, the air was fresh and invigorating, and when they at last dragged themselves indoors, Albert busied himself with the 'charming, though very simple' rosewood furniture which he had bought for the drawing room and for their rooms upstairs. With the new wallpaper, also chosen by Albert, his chintz sofas, 'china ornaments of all kinds we had by us', and many of their own pictures ('all, our *very* own, which makes it so doubly nice'[7]), old Osborne was already feeling like home. Albert spent the week, in his words, 'Building, demolishing, gardening and measuring'.[8] It was the beginning of a long process whereby Albert reversed the conditions that had prevailed when he married Victoria; they began their married life with everything that surrounded them belonging to her, at Osborne she came to be surrounded by everything that was chosen and arranged by him.

The important morning of 23 June 1845 dawned fine and windy. Shortly after breakfast Victoria, Albert and their two eldest children, Vicky and Bertie, went down the way which had been arranged for them into the foundations. Superintended by Mr Cubitt, a small glass box containing coins of the Queen's reign and an inscription recording those who were present, was placed in a hole in the ground and cemented over, which, the Queen recorded carefully, 'we and the children carried out'. Then the large foundation stone was placed over it and they all went round and hammered on it. The Queen added a short prayer to her account of these important events: 'I trust that God may bless this work and that we may live many happy years in the house, with our children and children's children and that many centuries may still see our descendents living there.'[9]

While Cubitt's workforce laboured at the foundations of her new home, the Queen's diary breathed a long summer of rural delights. Honeysuckle and

OPPOSITE: *King Leopold of the Belgians*, by Winterhalter, 1859. 'Dear kind Uncle,' wrote the Queen, 'always so aimiable, and whom I have *ever loved* as a *father*.' (RA QVJ, 23 July 1855)

The Rosenau, by Douglas Morison, 1845; the country residence of the Dukes of Coburg where Albert spent most of his boyhood.

dog roses twined in the hedgerows, wild flowers flourished in the fields, and the Queen wore wreaths of cornflowers in her hair at dinner. Albert found a cuttlefish on the beach and taught Victoria how this curious animal produced sepia. He was always teaching, moulding her, encouraging her to curb her temper; in many ways he was as much a father figure to her as he was husband; she in turn admired his knowledge and teaching, as she did everything about him.

They attended service in the little church at Whippingham which Victoria remembered well from her earlier visits to the island, and where the people behaved 'so nicely'. How pleasant it was to be able to get out so easily, and how lovely to walk through the woods with Albert, particularly now that small bridges were in place so that one no longer had to leap over the ditches, and to rest a while down on the shore where the high tide was as smooth and clear as glass. Uncle Leopold, visiting in July, tactfully found himself reminded of Italy by the myrtles and fine shrubs growing in the open air. The Queen's luncheon table was graced with wild strawberries from the woods, grapes and raspberries from her own kitchen garden. Blue sea, pure air, complete seclusion and the balm of ownership; all had 'a most beneficial and calming effect on one's mind and spirits'.[10] Even the visit of the King of the Netherlands hardly ruffled this island idyll. They lodged him in Norris Castle, which had been hired for the purpose, and entertained him at Osborne: 'Really', wrote the Queen, her emphases underlining her relief, 'our dinner party and reception of a foreign sovereign in this *little house here*, went off as well, as *other* receptions, elsewhere.'[11]

In August Victoria and Albert went to Germany leaving their children behind at Osborne. Travel abroad, especially to the homeland of her beloved husband, was a new experience for Victoria, deeply conscious that she was visiting the place which would have been her home had she not been Queen of England. They actually stayed at the '*dear Rosenau*', and the Queen saw for herself the plain little rooms on the top floor where Albert and his brother Ernest had been brought up and where the wallpaper was still full of holes from their fencing. She heard for herself the fountain in the courtyard, and was charmed with a small building within walking distance of the Rosenau, 'a regular Swiss Cottage, with pretty little rooms, one enters by an outside wooden staircase.'[12] Having visited some of the oldest parts of Coburg, they walked down to the new arcades in the gardens. Albert would have returned to

The room in the Rosenau occupied by Albert and his brother Ernest as children, by F. Rothbart. This is how it looked, the same as he remembered it, when Albert took Victoria there in 1845.

The bathing house at the Rosenau, by M. Bruckner, where Albert and Ernest learnt to swim.

Osborne with a fresh stimulus from his home, and like many exiles, he created for himself in his adoptive country echoes of the home he had left behind.

They returned to the Isle of Wight in September with numerous souvenirs from Germany to arrange round the house, and two 'dear little dächels', or dachshunds; the dogs were 'great fun', and 'so good with the children'. In the month Victoria and Albert had been away the new house had got on 'immensely', and the kitchen, at the back of the old house, as far as possible from the Queen's future dining room in the new house, was quite finished and already in use. 'It is said to be excellent', wrote the Queen at a regal distance from domesticity.[13]

The new house went up with astonishing speed, completely overtaking the lawyers' disputes with Lady Isabella over the value of crops, furniture, fixtures, drainage, and interest due on such sums. By the end of November 1845, with the ink of Lady Isabella's dilatory signature still wet on the deeds of sale, Queen Victoria, returning to Osborne after an absence of two months, was delighted to find that the new house had been 'quite built up', even as far as the tower, which was raised over the foundation stone.[14]

The new house, which came to be known as the Pavilion, was in an Italianate style. It would have suggested itself naturally to the Prince who had rounded off his education, 'intoxicated with delight', on a Grand Tour in Italy, and who had already bought some of the finest early Italian paintings ever to find their way to England, at a time when these 'primitives' were very unfashionable. The order and proportion of Palladian architecture attracted him; and it would have seemed natural to build an Italianate house appropriate to the wide sweep of sea and coastline which reminded him of the Bay of Naples. It is not possible to tell from the hints and scraps of paperwork which survive from the Prince's first great building project exactly how Albert was involved with the design. Long years afterwards, the Queen, a notorious partisan where her beloved angel was concerned, wrote that the house was planned by the Prince and 'most admirably carried out and executed' by Cubitt.[15] She may have been giving her husband more than his due credit; on the other hand Albert always threw himself passionately into the details of any project; this was his first, and a great deal of care went into the preparation of the plans, down to plaster casts which were made of the projected buildings and terraces.[16]

The concept may have been Albert's, but the Pavilion was clearly marked with Cubitt's townish stamp ('rather on a Londony plan', was how one of the Queen's ladies put it,[17] but countrified with the whimsy of a tower. The house would have seemed smart, elegant, even light-hearted – after all, it was a holiday house – and with its grandiose portico, and windows ornamented with pediments and Corinthian columns would have been thought a refreshing improvement on the old Osborne. This had had no pretentions to beauty in the eyes of Victoria's subjects, to whom the restraint and proportion of the eighteenth century had come to seem flat and insipid.

The Queen was relieved to find that the tower looked 'so well not at all too high';[18] since she herself accepted uncritically anything her husband did, this remark, implying that the design could fall short of complete perfection, may voice a doubt that Albert himself entertained. The view from the roof,

BELOW RIGHT: Albert sketched the Pavilion in a letter to his step-grandmother, Caroline, Duchess of Saxe-Coburg-Gotha, 29 November 1845, adding 'I fear this abominable drawing will give you a sorry opinion of it, but I assure you that it is very pretty, and I will send you a proper drawing of it one day.'

LEFT: By December 1845, when the *Illustrated London News* published this engraving, the new house was already dwarfing the old.

Wolfe's statue of Albert was put up on the nursery landing in August 1846. It became a focus for his youngest children to celebrate his birthday when he was not at Osborne, and they would lay posies at its naked feet. Photograph by Jabez Hughes.

when Albert took her up there, was 'really quite beautiful';[19] on a clear day she and her consort now had a magnificent panorama from this vantage point. To the east lay the whole anchorage of Spithead and the Motherbank; northwards, the Queen could see up Southampton Water with its transatlantic, peninsular and oriental steamers; she could see Cowes Roads, studded with ships; looking west, she had a view of the Solent, the New Forest and the Needles lighthouse; to the south, the Downs, the River Medina, the town of Newport, Albany Barracks and Carisbrooke Castle. Albert was giving her a new perspective, and was himself 'very content and happy'.[20]

Mr Cubitt took the Queen and Prince on a conducted tour of the Pavilion, which now had a staircase and ceilings. Albert began to think about furniture, to be supplied by Messrs Dowbiggin of London; the new house promised to be 'quite perfection' – the cares of state, which could not be entirely escaped even here, at least seemed easier to bear. In 1846 they visited Osborne on eight separate occasions, usually for a week or so, sometimes for as long as a fortnight; and the Queen would exclaim 'How enjoyable our life is here!'[21]

The Pavilion was already being embellished with statuary. On 15 August 1846 the Queen and Prince climbed the wide staircase up to the landing on the third floor outside the rooms which were to be the nurseries, to watch the installation in a large niche of a statue of Albert by the sculptor Wolfe, which Albert had given Victoria in 1841. It was a problematic piece. The Greek armour was quite acceptable, but the bare legs and feet made Albert – not

Victoria – decide it looked 'too undressed to place in a room'.[22] Albert hid away the offending legs on this quiet cul-de-sac outside the nurseries at the top of the house and commissioned another likeness, decently shod, from John Gibson, for Buckingham Palace.

Almost daily the Prince and Queen were over in the Pavilion, watching the progress of the work and arranging furniture and pictures; there was 'great bustle going on', said the Queen. At last, on the evening of 14 September 1846, all was ready. As the Queen entered the house for her first night there, one of her ladies-in-waiting, a Scot, threw an old shoe into the house after her for luck; 'it looked too strange and amusing', remarked one of the English ladies. They dined in the brilliant lamplight which for the first time shone through the windows far out to sea and after dinner the assembled company drank the health of the Queen and of the Prince, who quoted two lines of a hymn used in Germany on such occasions. 'It was dry and quaint, being Luther's', said Lady Lyttelton, 'but we all perceived that he was feeling it.' From now on, at Osborne at least, Albert was in an environment of his own choosing.

The new house was not designed to impress anyone with the wealth or dignity of a great sovereign. It was intended to be a comfortable home in a pleasant spot, so practicality (from the point of view, that is, of the royal family, rather than their Household and servants), and a modest grandeur where necessary, characterized the design of the Pavilion. All the rooms were grouped around the central staircase, which, very like the one at Claremont, was probably copied from it.[23] On the ground floor, from end to end of the north-east facade, facing the sea, stretched the drawing room. Royal eagerness was such that this room was not yet finished when they moved in. Victoria described the drawing room as 'a simple, yet at the same time handsome, room, with a

In July 1846 Edward Lear drew the Pavilion; he had come to Osborne to teach the Queen landscape painting.

bow to it'.[24] With its imitation marble pillars and plain, arched chimneypiece, it was the most formal room in the house, and was in fact designed to bend the rules, for round the corner was a billiard room divided from it only by columns, where the gentlemen of the Household, prevented by etiquette from sitting in Her Majesty's presence, could be on hand, but out of sight and so remain comfortably seated. This open-plan arrangement was unusual for its day. At the other end of the drawing room from the billiard room was the dining room. It too had tall bow windows which like those of the drawing room were glazed with the expensive new luxury of plate glass, all the better to enjoy the wonderful view.

The downstairs rooms were for entertaining guests, listening to concerts, even, when the occasion arose, dancing. Directly above them and commanding, if possible, an even finer view of the sea, lay the intimate suite which the Queen described as 'our living rooms, consisting of a bedroom (above the dining room), dressing room and bathroom (in one), our sitting room a lovely room, with a bow, very like the shape of mine at Buckingham Palace; opening out of that is Albert's dressing room, and leading out of that his bathroom.'[25] There was nothing grand at all about these rooms. They were intimate and convenient. Husband and wife each enjoyed the rare luxury of his or her own bath with hot water from a furnace deep in the bowels of the basement. Each had a water closet, the Queen's accessible from her bedroom and her dressing room, and discreetly disguised as part of a vast built-in wardrobe. Beside the big tester bed in their bedroom was an ingenious mechanism whereby the door could be locked without having to get out of bed.

Above the parents' apartments were the children's, and rooms for some of the Queen's maids, conveniently close to their mistress. 'All is so convenient, spacious, and well-carried out', wrote the Queen. 'Mr Cubitt has done it admirably. He is such an honest, kind good man. It appears to me like a dream to be here now in our own house, of which we laid the first stone only 15 months ago!' Once again, she called for 'God's blessing on our new house, and all its inmates and may he allow us to enjoy it in peace and comfort for many years to come.'[26]

The Queen thought that her new house was 'beautifully and most solidly built'.[27] Some of her purist subjects would have disagreed, for it was not built of stone, which would have been prohibitively expensive, but of bricks, set in mortar, the exterior covered in stucco, moulded and coloured to imitate stone. Portland stone was used only for important areas where a touch of grandeur suitable to the Queen's dignity was appropriate: the portico over the Queen's entrance, the paving in the corridors on the ground floor, and the staircase. The windows, too, were subtly graded; good quality materials were used throughout, but the best were reserved for the royal apartments. The house was more remarkable for its thoughtful design and attention to detail – so characteristic of Albert's methods – from the lead sinks in the basement to the spiral staircase up to the flagtower, than for a lavish or indiscriminate use of expensive materials. The Queen and Prince did not require the same excesses as her uncle George IV.

Fire was a very real hazard in a house warmed by open fires and lit by oil lamps; but in their new house the royal family enjoyed the invisible benefits of Cubitt's so-called 'fireproof construction', a technique which had developed from late eighteenth-century factories and warehouses, whereby the massive

Primroses grew thickly in the woods of Osborne, and always held a special association for the Queen, who often painted the flowers of Osborne.

During their first week in the new house, in September 1846, Victoria and Albert painted the view from their new sitting room. Perhaps it was Albert who included the balustrade and the curtains for when the Queen worked alone she did not 'frame' her landscapes like this.

brick arches and iron girders which supported the floors were constructed so that even if the most heavily furnished room were to catch fire it could not spread, up, down, or into the room next door. Her Majesty's marine residence was insulated, for sound as well as fire, with crushed sea shells.

They had moved from the old house to the new with barely a week left of their visit. 'It is rather royal', remarked Lady Lyttelton drily, 'to move with all the risks of paint and discomfort for so very few days.'[28] The Queen sat at the French windows in her sitting room, and began the first of many sketches of the view, 'the sea so blue and calm and the sails of the boats cruising about, so dazzlingly white. We are miserable at having to leave this Paradise, with this perfect house, so soon.'[29]

While the Queen sketched or worked at the contents of her red despatch boxes, there was work for Albert in the pleasure grounds. Alongside the old house Cubitt's men had already begun to dig the foundations of the large service wing, later known as the Household Wing, activity which necessitated a good deal of what the Queen called 'arranging', mostly in the form of transplanting some of the huge, much-admired myrtles and evergreens, 'a tremendous job', said the Queen; 'one myrtle required fifteen men to move it!'[30] The evergreens 'removed from the old house', as she put it, were planted 'along the path there is to be to the sea'.[31] Evergreens were also put in at Barton.

Autumn and winter, the seasons of tree planting, had now become a

A pen and ink sketch of Osborne, by Prince Albert, 1849.

particularly busy time for Albert, who would often be out almost all day planning and directing; even the Queen found she had a new interest: 'After luncheon we were out for nearly two hours, I, helping Albert with his planting, which I found very entertaining.'[32] As well as the wide belts of woodland trees which he staked out to provide shelter and privacy and a carefully composed panorama of field, wood and sea, Albert dared to plant in the mild island air some of the rarities which were only just arriving from all over the world, sometimes they were some of the first specimens available. Some he bought, some were given to him and the pleasure grounds and garden filled up with his choice plants. In March 1846, walking up and down under the wall of the pleasure ground, the Queen watched her 'dearest Albert plant a daphne, a magnolia, and two Nerpoles Japonica, very rare and exotic-looking plants, which hardly ever grow out of doors with us, – and on the grass,' added the Queen, botany deserting her, 'a Chinese plant. Albert got himself into such a heat, by working away so hard himself.'[33] She herself decorously planted a tulip tree in the pleasure grounds.

Albert had an able lieutenant in Andrew Toward, his Land Steward, who had previously been in the service of Queen Victoria's aunt, the Duchess of Gloucester, at Bagshot Park. Toward had been at Osborne nearly as long as Victoria and Albert, having been appointed in August 1845, and was deeply involved with all Albert's projects on the estate, from tree planting to sewage filtration. The relationship between the two men was cordial and creative, Albert had confidence in, and a great liking for, his 'indefatigable' steward under whom everything, road-making, buildings, landscaping, was 'always well and most judiciously carried out'.[34]

The Prince would be out whole mornings transplanting, which after a season or two his wife, in a rare fit of criticism, accused him of being too fond of doing. The trees transformed the place. Oaks, and rhododendrons – those Himalayan exotica whose glossy dark leaves were such a favourite with Victorians – were planted behind the kitchen garden, and screened the kitchens and other 'offices' from view. An avenue of Guernsey elms went in at Barton, whole turnip fields were swallowed up by plantations, a sheltering screen of trees and shrubs was planted behind the Landing House down on the shore and large bay trees established in the pleasure grounds around the house.

Ornamenting and improving was very labour intensive. Initially eleven men, and a boy who weeded, worked in the gardens and pleasure grounds; but later the number leapt to twenty-five, reflecting the extensive acreage of terraces and flower gardens, the increased proportion of land now devoted to

The Queen's dressing room, by James Roberts, 1851. Her bath was hidden away behind the mirrors on the left. The decoration, the curtains and carpets, the furniture, and most of the pictures were all, as throughout the house, chosen by Albert.

trees, and the importance of the kitchen gardens. The melon grounds, heated greenhouses, grapehouses, fruit rooms and potting rooms were no ornaments but were expected to provide produce for the royal table.

Victoria and Albert returned to Osborne in November. 'We found our rooms very comfortable', said the Queen, 'though cold.' Lady Lyttelton, now the children's governess, also found that her rooms were cold and draughty. On Albert's orders, Mr Cubitt called on her, and 'in a profusion of promises of making every effort to cure the evil, and of attending to its symptoms, he said "I will not neglect any hint of your ladyship's. I will *go the length of believing every word you say about it*".'[35]

The drawing room now looked extremely handsome with its yellow damask satin curtains and furniture to match. When they dined in company, and played patience in the drawing room after dinner it looked to the Queen 'really beautiful, with the chandeliers lighted and all our fine presents to each other of pictures, statuary, furniture and "objets d'art". All harmonizes so well together.'[36] It was equally delightful to dine alone with Albert and afterwards to be 'snug in our charming sitting room'.

In March 1847 the soft furnishing of the drawing room was completed with an Aubusson carpet, specially woven to fit round the columns. The billiard table was in place, too. Designed by Albert himself, made by Magnus and decorated by Thurston, it was in keeping with the house and was Italianate in style. Its eight slate legs were straight, and painted to imitate marble, while around the side panels ran a Florentine pattern in green, orange and gold. Billiard balls clicked and rolled across the level surface under the light cast by the lamp hanging above it, also of the Prince's own designing. 'Really the effect of the whole is charming',[37] said his wife, and tried her hand at a game or two.

Everywhere pictures were beginning to go up; Franz Xaver Winterhalter's portrait of Albert, 'painted with the peculiar effect of sunshine' which the Queen so admired, was hung in their sitting room. A gallery of ancestors and relations, all depicted as children, were carried up to the top floor and installed in the schoolroom. Albert spent an afternoon hanging his Renaissance paintings in his study–dressing room next door to the Queen's sitting room. In all, there were about twenty-five early Italian and German paintings which he had acquired through his artistic adviser, Ludwig Gruner, at much the same time as Osborne was being built. They were by far the best paintings at Osborne (and are now in the National Gallery), but Albert hung many of them away from public view, in the only room which he shared with no one else.

By May 1847 the roof of the Household Wing was complete. The Queen, comfortably at home in the Pavilion whose progress she had watched with breathless expectancy, took a less keen interest in what was really service accommodation for her Court, and rather vaguely pronounced the new wing to be 'very nice and full of charming rooms'.[38]

In July the terrace in front of the Pavilion was completed. It had been a major, and expensive, undertaking which required massive earth-moving and a fortress-like retaining wall, all now hidden below the standard bay trees, the flowerbeds, brightly planted with geraniums and stocks and fragrant heliotrope, and the balustrade which made such a 'charming effect' with the sea behind it. Here was an elegant promenade, to walk upon before dressing for

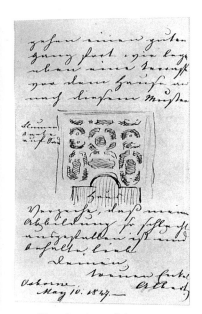

Sketch-plan of the terrace, drawn by Prince Albert in a letter to his step-grandmother, 10 May 1847.

dinner, to sit out upon after dinner, even to dance upon, when there happened to be a band and a splendid moonlit night.

The Queen worked diligently at her accomplishments. Tempted by the vistas of wood and sea, she had taken up landscape painting the previous summer, when Mr Edward Lear, of the nonsense rhymes and limpid watercolour landscapes, came to Osborne to give her some lessons. He had been lavish with praise and encouragement so the Queen concluded that he taught remarkably well. She was full of admiration for his drawings at Osborne, and had a vignette engraved from one of them. Traces of his influence endured in her work. Her long-term drawing master, however, was Mr William Leighton Leitch, who became a regular visitor. She was engagingly modest about her watercolours. In the privacy of her diary she could allow that she had just finished a view of Osborne 'really I must own, very nicely, considering that I only started sketching in July';[39] but when she showed her paintings to a professional artist visiting Osborne, she made deprecating reference to her 'daubs'. She chose to paint subjects which delighted her: the new vistas which

Prince Albert's dressing room, by James Roberts, 1851. On the walls are his treasured Italian paintings; to the left is a glimpse through to the Queen's sitting room; to the right, in his bathroom, is a fresco depicting Hercules and Omphale: the hero in thrall to the enchantress.

Osborne under construction, by W. L. Leitch, August 1847. The Pavilion had been completed for over a year; the Household Wing built, and the Main Wing planned on the site of the old house (hidden behind the trees). The rampart-like terraces were taking shape, and lawns being levelled.

Albert was creating at Osborne, both the building itself, and the views from it. She never painted the interior, and she very rarely painted Albert, although page after page of her sketchbooks were filled with representations of his children.

Luigi Lablache came down from London to give her singing lessons. This enormous Neapolitan, half-French, half-Irish, who must have towered over his diminutive royal pupil, was the most famous bass of his generation and an entertaining singing master. He spiced his tutorials with gossip about the latest operatic scandals, being 'very funny', said the Queen, at the expense of Verdi's latest opera (*I masnadieri*, the only opera Verdi wrote for London, had opened at Her Majesty's Theatre on 22 July), and agreed with Victoria and Albert that it was 'really very bad'; and had they heard that Covent Garden was ruined and that the Persianis and Salvé had been obliged to run away? One of his visits included the 'real treat' of an informal concert with Jenny Lind, known as the 'Swedish Nightingale', to whom the Queen gave a bracelet and expressed her admiration for the singer's wonderful talent. Miss Lind, as talented a courtier as she was a singer, replied that the Queen's words of appreciation meant even more to her than the present.

The Queen tried new experiences too. On 30 July she drove down to the beach with her maid and climbed into the bathing machine, a small wooden hut on wheels, which allowed her to undress in private. The machine was run out into the water, where the Queen descended the steps and took her first sea bathe, with a 'very nice' bathing woman in attendance. 'I thought it delightful', she said, 'till I put my head under water, when I thought I should be stifled.'[40] The next time she was more cautious, sponging her head before she 'plunged about'. One fine evening there was a fishing expedition. The royal party embarked on a small fishing boat in the charge of an old man and a boy who rowed them out beyond Norris Castle, where they anchored and let down their lines. 'We were most successful in our fishing attempts', wrote the Queen, 'and might have caught more had our bait been smaller and better.' The party caught thirty-nine whiting (of which the Queen caught ten), a conger eel and a dog fish. 'We all got rather wet', she admitted, 'pulling up and letting down the lines. Walked up to the house a little before 8 having had a most amusing afternoon.'[41] The old man and the boy enjoyed their afternoon too, and must have had many a drink on the strength of the Queen's catch, which a decade later, the story being retailed to a frankly incredulous visitor, had grown to thirteen and a half dozen of that mysterious fish, the 'whiting trout'.

It was one of the rare summers when the Queen was not pregnant, and on several evenings when visitors were staying the carpet in the drawing room would be taken up and the company would dance quadrilles and country dances. They were careful on a Saturday to end their revels by midnight, for although the Queen disapproved of the long tedium of the Sabbatarian Sunday, she would never have allowed herself to dance on the Lord's Day.

From July to October, under the marble gaze of the statue of Albert at the top of the stairs in the Pavilion, there was a project under way which interested Albert 'most deeply, and everybody a little – Mr Dyce at his fresco picture'.[42] William Dyce was one of the few artists in England at that time who was capable of tackling the ancient art of fresco, painting straight into wet plaster in

Fresco by William Dyce, 1847, at the top of the Pavilion staircase, depicting Neptune, the king of the sea, handing his crown to Britannia. Victoria and Albert were delighted with his work; the Queen's Ladies were inclined to feel shocked at such naked display.

the short time before it dries. He had done one of the fresco panels in the garden pavilion at Buckingham Palace, an early brainchild of Albert's, and was also involved in the frescoes which formed part of the decorations of the new Houses of Parliament. He was adorning the wall at the top of the staircase in the Pavilion with a compliment appropriate to Her Majesty's marine residence. It shows Neptune in a chariot drawn by three white horses in a sea foaming with lusty tritons and well-fleshed mermaids, offering his crown to Britannia, who stands on the shore among a group of emblematic figures, only some of whom are wearing clothes. She herself is swathed in red and gold draperies, one hand holding a trident, the other resting on the head of her lion which glares suspiciously, even hungrily, at the sea-king's entourage. The Queen was full of admiration for 'a magnificent painting, so well-drawn, conceived and executed'.[43] Her less broad-minded ladies were disconcerted by the nudity of these deities all 'in the Royal Africa, minus the boots'; however, pigment alleviated the impropriety: 'as the skins are all dark mahogany colour, it looks so unnatural that one does not feel it very shocking.'[44]

Rooms and corridors in the Pavilion were becoming peopled with statuary of a classical air, the beginnings of a collection which was to become one of the most substantial in England. It already included *Narcissus*, by William Theed, a replica of the statue at Anglesey Abbey (the difference being that the one at Osborne preserved his modesty with a fig leaf), and R. J. Wyatt's creamy marble *Glycera*, maker of garlands, which stood by the dining-room door. Also, in the drawing room life-sized marmorean cherubs appeared on pedestals of red Cornish marble. These were the four eldest children, the Princess Royal, as *Summer*, the Prince of Wales as *Winter* with a dog and shepherd's crook, Princess Alice as *Spring*, and the two-year-old Prince Alfred clutching a bunch of grapes as *Autumn* (some people strongly disapproved of this reference to the demon drink). They were all by one of the very few women sculptors of the nineteenth century, Mary Thornycroft. 'They look so well', said the Queen, 'and are such good likenesses.'[45]

The Household Wing was now at an advanced stage. The Queen declared it to be 'delightful, so warm, yet airy, and very comfortable'.[46] Like the Pavilion, this substantial building had gone up with astonishing speed, over a period of some fifteen months and was really another self-contained house ultimately to be connected to the Pavilion by the long sculpture gallery, though until that was built the Queen's ladies had to take a 'little run in the open air' to reach the Pavilion. On the ground floor was the dining room for the Household, a library, a billiard room, the Master of the Household's room, the equerries' room, even another bathroom with the apparatus of furnaces and cisterns to supply hot running water, and the Smoking Room, the only room in the house which did not have the initials 'V' and 'A' lovingly entwined over the door; here was just a lonely 'A', even though Albert did not smoke.

Upstairs on each floor a long corridor ran the considerable length of the building; opening off it were bedrooms and sitting rooms for the various members of the Household and for visitors. The building was heated by a volcanic furnace deep in the basement which flushed hot air out through ornamental grilles in the corridors; individual rooms still enjoyed the benefits and disadvantages of open fires in the plain fireplaces supplied by Cubitt's workshops. Central heating was not unheard of at this time; but it was one of

the progressive features of the house. It was perhaps to minimize the danger of fire from the heating system, as well as to keep costs down, that the skirting 'boards' were actually made of moulded cement.

At the end of 1847, Victoria and Albert took leave of the old Osborne House, now sandwiched between the Pavilion and the Household Wing, and about to be demolished to make way for the Main Wing. The Queen felt a certain sadness looking at their old rooms 'just as they were, so snug and comfortable, and still just as if ready for us. For two years we were so happy in them, as it was our first *own* little *home*. Those poor rooms will *all* be pulled down, as soon as we leave!'[47]

Cubitt put blinds on the windows of the Pavilion to keep the dust out, carefully saved some fixtures such as cupboards and fireplaces to be used again, and the front door with its fanlight which was to be set into the garden wall (where it may still be seen today), and used the bricks and rubble of the old

The sculpture corridor, by James Roberts, 1852. This watercolour captures the atmosphere that Albert worked so hard to create: the neoclassical statues he chose look down on three children and a dachshund, who are perhaps on their way down to the seashore beyond the open window.

View from the Queen's sitting room, which she painted on 22 July 1849. Throughout the month, she had been taking lessons from William Leitch.

house to build the new wing. When the Queen returned in the spring of 1848 she found that she did not miss the old house much, as the Main Wing was going up so fast. Later, however, she and Albert, while admitting that they had 'quite outgrown' old Osborne and could not have continued living there, did regret that the character of the old house had gone.[48]

The Household Wing was ready for furnishing and garnishing. Albert, as always, went to great pains. Months earlier he had inspected the pictures, china and ornaments which they already had in store and had haunted the new rooms to work out where furniture and ornaments from the old house could go, and how much new furniture they would need. One morning in April 1848 two of the Queen's ladies-in-waiting, quietly settled in their drawing room, were caught up in the whirlwind:

... in walked the Prince to see how our rooms were arranged for the third time, and to look at what spaces there were for pictures; we consulted with him for two hours or more, running up and down stairs, measuring panels, and discussing the respective merits of the different pictures. He walked into all our rooms, going, however, through the ceremony of asking our leave; and looking at all our arrangements, and on the whole, very agreeable, seeming so pleased at working himself, pushing the piano, tables, etc, about to see how they would look best.[49]

It speaks volumes for the efficiency of Cubitt and his workforce that the Queen found Osborne, which for the past three years had been one vast building site, a peaceful place to be. The army of masons, plasterers, stone hewers and carpenters to whom Albert always enjoyed talking,[50] laboured on through all the royal visits. While the new buildings went up, all kinds of odd jobs needed doing in and around the Pavilion. Until the permanent staff necessary to the running of another royal establishment were put in place, these tasks fell to Cubitt's workforce, and give us an idea of the amount, and variety, of labour involved in the creation of a tranquil royal retreat. Cubitt's workmen cleaned birds' nests out of drainpipes and gutters, and put in gratings to stop the

Osborne under construction, pencil sketch by W. L. Leitch. Albert always enjoyed talking to the workmen who were building Osborne.

birds doing it again. They removed temporary landings, paving, and stairs; they cleared dust out of drains and regularly cleaned the windows and the stone pavements and steps round the house; they repaired garden seats and shears; they improved the well on the lawn, carried water to various parts of the house while the alteration was being made, and pumped water into cisterns; they fetched, repaired, and set up the stands for the band on the terrace; they put up tents and marquees, took them down again, and shipped them to London; they weathered off stone bases for pedestals on the terraces and rigged the flagstaff with new halyards.

Indoors all kinds of work came their way: they swept flues and chimneys, beat carpets, cleaned grease out of the dining-room floor and repolished the oak floor in the drawing room; they repaired the paint in the principal rooms and in the water closet off the Queen's bedroom; they repaired the bell pull in her sitting room; they painted her shower bath; they painted Albert's shower bath; they cleaned cornices, marble chimneypieces and looking glasses; they repaired plaster on the back stairs damaged by luggage; they repaired skylights and plaster figures; they painted stone sinks, wooden pedestals and iron pipes and gratings; they adjusted bath and sink apparatus, and eased sticking doors; they made packing cases, a chest for a lapidary's tools, a folding screen covered in figured paper for the sleeping room in the basement; they made a pair of steps for mounting a saddle horse; they painted a toy barrow; lined and distempered archery targets; delivered 3 lb. of lead to the Prince's Jäger, or personal outdoor servant, for casting bullets; made a strong deal chest for a gun case, and a board for children's amusements in the drawing room; they even, briefly, took up arms in the defence of their sovereign.

The year 1848 was marked by foul weather, revolutions in Europe and Chartist unrest in England. Ripples of alarm spread even as far as Osborne and on 13 June, the Queen recorded in her diary:

There was an alarm, which however ended in nothing, of 40 Chartists having come over to Cowes, with the intention of coming up here. In an instant all Cubitt's men and all our labourers armed with sticks, were placed in readiness. The sailors from the *Fairy* came up with carbines, some troops were sent for from Parkhurst, who arrived in two hours time, all was in battle array, but it ended in nothing. The suspected people belonged, it seems to a company of 'Odd Fellows' who had come to enjoy themselves on Whit Tuesday, and it happened that two notable Chartists had been seen by the police, and had been rude in their questions at the lodge. This was all that caused the alarm – when we walked out in the evening, we saw the small company of troops march away from Barton.

Other than this isolated incident, the seclusion of Osborne gave the Court a very real sense of security and liberty. There had already been attempts on the Queen's life, and there was always a discreet police presence, in the person of a constable or two, at Osborne. One of the Queen's ladies wrote home much amused at the difference between Windsor and Osborne. 'Here we may pleasure about in every direction, even along the public roads, they are so quiet, and we think nothing of *tête à tête* walks, a thing that would make everybody's hair stand on end at Windsor.'[51]

The terrible weather did little to dampen royal enjoyment, but the days were rare when Victoria could be out with her sketchbooks, sitting on a stone by

View from the unfinished terrace, by W. L. Leitch and Lady Canning, August 1848. Albert chose strong colours for the garden, just as he had for his interiors.

the sea while Albert went partridge shooting, and as often as not she was forced to take her walk in one of the long new corridors. Leitch came to the island with paints and flattery, and Lablache with gossip of Sicilian politics. The Queen, her children, and her ladies, took carriage exercise in the charabanc, a vehicle in which whoever sat in the second seat had to manage the drag, or brake, when going downhill. Descent of steep places when the Queen happened to be sitting there could be alarming, as she would talk so much she would forget to apply the drag, and no one would dare remind her. These were informal excursions, and if a canary in the street at Ryde caught her fancy she would stop to buy it.

By November 1848 the clock tower at the end of the Main Wing was finished. The Queen thought it very pretty but Albert was not satisfied. He installed a clock from Kew, which had belonged to George III. The hands were not right, so he went to characteristically painstaking and cost-conscious lengths to alter them. They were to be made of copper and gilded, but rather than make expensive alterations in the metal, first he had the hands traced out full-size on paper; he made several alterations which were incorporated in mock-ups cut out of wood and painted yellow to simulate a gilded finish and only when he had altered and approved the wooden version were the copper hands cut and gilded. Just as the hands did not please his demanding eye, so the chimes jarred on his musical ear and he had some of the three bells recast to give a deeper sound.[52]

Meanwhile, great earthworks were under way in front of the Main Wing. In July 1848 Albert, with Ludwig Gruner and Cubitt, had laid out a new terrace. The lawn in front of the house had to be lowered, 'a great job', said the Queen when she saw it in March 1849, 'but admirably carried out'. The terrace in front of the Pavilion was adorned in July 1849, the Queen reported, with a 'large flower vase, which is filled with flowers. The paths also have all been fresh

Terrace at the Rosenau, photograph by Frances Bedford, 1857. At Osborne, Albert echoed the gardens of his boyhood with similar balustrading, urns planted with yuccas, and fountains.

gravelled and it is impossible to see a prettier terrace.'[53] But when the new one was finished the impossible became possible, being, she said, so 'prettily and tastefully laid out. It gives such a finish to the whole place, and makes it look so much larger.'[54] When all the stonework had been done, Andrew Toward put 'all the good earth', the topsoil, back along the bottom of the wall and in several of the beds, and took delivery of a cargo of 'bog mould' from the New Forest for Albert's acid-loving camelias, azaleas, and rhododendrons.[55] With all their steps, balustrades, recesses and arches, these terraces were not an English garden; the inspiration was Italianate, via Coburg – the three arches, for instance, recalling the arcades in the gardens which both the royal couple had seen on their visit there in 1845.

With his eye on a distant horizon, Albert put in trees associated with nobility and longevity, evergreen oaks, bays, and the difficult cork oak. He thinned the wood going down to the sea and planted 500 'fine and rare trees'. Effective drainage was essential; Cubitt's brick kilns on the Newport Road turned out drainage tiles by the half-million and long before Albert had finished 126 miles of drains had already been laid all over the estate.

The house was nearing completion, but Albert was still completely 'wrapt up in all his creations here, his plants, his buildings etc.',[56] creating a vast mound near the house which disguised a reservoir, and planting it up, and occupied with Gruner over what the Queen called the 'architectural parts of

The Venus fountain, by the Queen, 1852, who wrote in her journal on 18 May 1853 that it 'plays every day now and it is so delicious hearing it. We have the windows open all day and it is most lovely. Oh! if it could always remain like this and could time only be arrested.'

the other house'.[57] She admired the 'Italian looking' colonnade which now connected the Household Wing, the Main Wing and the Pavilion. But it was not enough just to beautify the house within and without, paying tribute to the muses with music and art; in a community where more than a hundred people were living, the goddess Hygiene demanded her own pungent libation and in the winter of 1849 and the summer of 1850 Albert applied his energies to 'some means of employing the sewage, for the purpose of manure',[58] and spent some time experimenting with a filtration process – the Queen deciding to sketch while her beloved was thus occupied.

The Illustrated London News, which came out every week and kept its readers abreast of the latest in politics, high society, fashion, and sensational disaster, published engravings of Her Majesty's marine residence, drawing its readers' attention to the 'tasteful character of the scene' and the 'elegant taste evident in the layout and improvement of the grounds'. Cubitt's contract came to an end with the year. His carpenters packed up their workshops and the stonemasons their saws; only the sea breeze stirred in the woods and a new silence fell over Osborne. The Queen found it 'quite strange no longer hearing any noise of workmen, which we had to accustom ourselves to for the last four years or more, – from the earliest hours of the morning.'[59]

Work, however, had by no means finished. To create a 'place' meant more than a house and gardens. It also meant the farm and the estate, in which Albert took such a keen interest. Barton Farm, a field away from Osborne, was an integral part of the whole. Repair, or rather, restoration, of its large Elizabethan manor house was amongst the earliest work that Albert had set in hand in 1845, work that needed doing urgently, for damp and leaks had left only seven out of twenty bedrooms habitable, and the accommodation was

On 16 August 1855, the Queen wrote in her journal: 'Sat out under the trees, where it was really heavenly, and sketched. Every day, every year, this dear sweet spot seems more lovely and with its brilliant sunshine, deep blue sea and dazzling flowers, is a perfect Paradise, – and all, my beloved one's creation, – the result of his exquisite taste.'

Aug: 16. 1855.

Barton Farm under reconstruction, *Illustrated London News*, 28 June 1845. Albert restored the neglected Elizabethan Manor House to provide extra rooms for gentlemen of the Court and accommodation for the Land Steward.

needed for gentlemen of the Court (even Queen Victoria's mother was to stay there before her suite was ready in the Main Wing of Osborne itself). The whole project bears Albert's stamp, and must be one of the earliest examples of Victorian restoration, sympathetically carried out. His buildings, from the baronial pinnacles of Balmoral to the humblest farm-labourer's cottage, were always sensitive to their surroundings and purpose. Barton was completely re-roofed and all the main features, architectural and decorative, were painstakingly restored. In Cubitt's kilns new bricks were fired, exact copies of the originals, which were used to rebuild the handsome old chimney stacks and the ornamental gables. Andrew Toward and his family lived at Barton, where ten bedrooms were reserved for the Court and had to be kept in readiness for use at short notice.

The farmstead was in no better condition than the house: tumbledown outbuildings, rotten gates, broken fencing, neglected land, mismanaged woods of oak and hazel. Albert set out to create a model farm at Barton, following Scottish principles of farming. He had the land drained and fertilized, and when the construction of Osborne House and terraces was finished, fine new farm buildings were begun at Barton and the outlying farms of Kingston, Heathfield, and Alverstone. The buildings at Barton came into operation in 1852, and were 'most useful'.

From the first, Albert made substantial investments in livestock, implements, manure and poultry, soon followed by all the necessary, and traditional,

Barton Farm, by W. L. Leitch, 1850. It was always a favourite spot for sketching parties.

chaff-cutting machines, oil-cake crushers, oat bruisers, clod crushers, sack-weighing machines and scarifiers. Albert's interest in new methods introduced some of the latest machinery too; in 1851 a haymaking machine was in use and the same summer he consulted William Cubitt, son of Thomas Cubitt, about a steam-engine which the Queen saw in action the following year, making 'a tremendous noise'.[60] Although the farm machinery was very up-to-date, its use on the land was still in its infancy and horse-power was provided by the great Clydesdales which came from Scotland in 1845, whose shining brass harness ornaments were among the first of Toward's purchases.

The farm grew wheat, oats, mangolds, ryegrass, and once the diminutive Queen, who stood barely five-foot tall, found herself going across 'and positively through, some of our barley fields, which were up to my waist!'[61] The farm became a great attraction on royal walks, whether as a nursery excursion or for the entertainment of distinguished guests. They would stop to look at the sheep being washed or shorn, and there were always pretty calves to admire in the spring. The Queen particularly enjoyed the harvest, a feeling that never left her through her long life, and she would always pay an annual visit to the rickyard to see it filling: 'all looking so lovely, the golden fields, the rich sheaves, and the carts loading, with a background of deep blue sky and sea. It looks so peaceful and abundant.'[62]

Victoria's interest in the farm was frankly sentimental; Albert's was practical, but one of his experiments particularly appealed to her. In 1848 Captain Cunninghame, the East India Company's Commissioner on the Tibet frontier, had obtained a small flock of 'Tibetan' sheep, native to the district of Ladakh, and reputedly very hardy and able to survive on poor food. The East India Company sent the flock from Calcutta to the Zoological Gardens in

Farm buildings at Barton, photograph by A. Disderi, 1867. The farm was a popular stopping place on royal walks, particularly when Victoria and Albert were out with their children.

Regent's Park. They were distributed to a handful of experimentally-minded landed proprietors with a view to improving the breed of hill sheep in England. A ram and three ewes arrived at Osborne in March 1849. The Queen was intrigued by their small size, tameness, flop ears and goat-like beards, and gave them names: Ranjeet Singh, Rance, Tibetta, and Sultana. Three lambs were born in May 1849. It was thought that the sheep would do well at Balmoral.

In general, the quality of Albert's livestock was high. He established a herd of exceptional Alderney cattle, a flock of South Down sheep, and excellent pigs. Toward was expected to keep a careful account of the farm's profitability, and the Queen was soon confiding to her journal that 'we have 92 lambs and nearly 600 sheep, which is very profitable, though I own I am not up to much in these agricultural details.'[63] The farm did well all round. A prize-winning Clydesdale stallion stood at stud there, and in 1858 Albert wrote to his eldest son, Bertie, from Osborne: 'I gained two first prizes at the Smithfield show for Downs and a second prize for pigs and had a Hereford bullock highly commended. Have I not reason to be proud as an agriculturalist?'[64]

In 1850 W. Keyl painted the Victoria cow and her offspring. She had been one of four cows presented to the Queen in 1846 by the people of Guernsey after the royal visit to the island. Beyond, are the Tibet sheep, brought from Ladakh in 1848.

When Victoria and Albert bought the estate of Osborne, they in effect bought the lives and fortunes, or rather, welfare, of the people living and working there. Although the islanders were never to occupy quite the same niche in her romantic heart as the Highlanders, they recommended themselves from the first, as the Queen noted on one of her earliest visits to her new property: 'The few people one meets (real good peasants) are most unobtrusive.'[65] She soon discovered that with landownership came the gratifying obligations of benevolence: 'I take such an interest in all our labourers and people here, also their children, and hope that when their cottages are in better order, I may be able to go and see them, which, with two or three exceptions, I cannot easily do now.'[66]

Initially, there were thirty-one cottages on the estate, for the most part occupied by the farm labourers and in a very bad state of repair. Families of six and seven were crammed into two rooms in 'miserable' cottages; 'they are certainly very small and uncomfortable', agreed the Queen.[67] Improving them became part and parcel of Albert's aspirations as a model agriculturalist. To begin with, in the late 1840s, Cubitt mended pumps, kitchen ranges, windows and roofs, replastered, repaired, and repainted. Later, some cottages were

simply torn down and rebuilt. The work continued for many years until eventually there were thirty-six cottages divided into sixty-one separate dwellings. Although conditions were considerably improved, they were still primitive; the cottage 'necessaries' being still 'mere holes' as late as 1880.[68] As was the standard practice, the tenants were each allowed to keep a pig (the gamekeeper was also allowed a cow), and to work a garden or allotment, to supplement what they earned.

Conditions of work on Osborne differed little from farms the length and breadth of England. A careful eye was kept on local rates of pay, as a rise at Osborne would affect the whole district. In other ways, however, the labourers were better off than the average. In August 1846, for instance, many labourers were dismissed, to enable them to work the harvest for other employers, all being told that the moment they were out of employment, they were to return to Osborne, where there would 'without fail' be work for them. Albert built a school for their children, which opened at Whippingham in 1850. Messrs Hoffmeister and Cass, who had a practice in Cowes, were paid an annual retainer by the Queen to look after the sick at Osborne, and there was also an estate nurse. When men fell sick they could expect sick-pay until they recovered

Ann Fleming, a daughter of the shepherd at Barton, painted by the Queen. In July 1849 Victoria went over to Barton three times to sketch the shepherd's daughters in the porch of their cottage.

Prince Albert's design for an estate cottage; by the time he had finished all his improvements, his tenants were well-housed and cared for.

Keeper's Lodge, Alverstone Gate, by W. L. Leitch, 1860. Besides a house, the gamekeeper was provided with fuel, a livery coat every year, a gun, and keep for the dogs.

Whippingham Church, by S. F. Prosser, 1845. It was to be rebuilt later by Albert.

or were buried (and the Queen would often contribute to funeral expenses), whereas on most estates, a man would think himself lucky to get half pay for a few weeks.

Victoria and Albert looked after their people from the cradle to the grave. Many details of the estate and its administration could have been delegated, but the royal couple always considered Osborne to be entirely under their personal control;[69] and it was one of its most potent charms that here normal channels of procedure did not operate, and officialdom was bypassed. The Queen summed up what she and her husband felt in her journal on 12 December 1847:

We agreed that we could never be thankful enough to have got this place, which is the source of such comfort, quiet, independence, amusement, enjoyment and occupation. The pure, refreshing air, is also so good for the health. All this repays us 1000 times for our expenses here.

CHAPTER THREE

A PLACE OF ONE'S OWN

While the Queen and Prince were away, Osborne seemed to hold its breath, and the only sounds were bird song and the sea breeze blowing through the trees. Then a letter, in later years a telegram, would arrive, warning of Her Majesty's imminent return. The sense of anticipation was palpable; the house was 'alert and rattling'; all doors were opened, rooms brightened up, and the musical clock began to chime. In due course, if the wind was in the right direction, anyone standing on the terrace could have heard the guns firing the salute as the Queen embarked at Gosport and soon the royal yacht, the *Victoria and Albert*, or the smaller *Fairy*, could be seen coming across the Solent, flying the royal standard. If the tide permitted, Victoria and Albert would put into Osborne Bay, and come ashore in the barge, perhaps walking up to the house through the woods. Otherwise, they would steam straight to Cowes and land at the new Trinity Pier, built in 1845 by the admiralty especially for Her Majesty's private use. From here, after 1854 when the principal entrance was finished, the royal party drove in at the imposing gates and up the avenue of ilex that led from the pier to the house, past the statues of a pair of antlered stags, and approached the house as Albert and Cubitt had intended, with the long colonnade in front of them and the Pavilion to their left. As the Queen entered the Pavilion, the blue, red and gold royal standard would be run up the flagstaff on the tower above, harps and lions fluttering and snapping in the sea winds.

These crossings and arrivals, after perhaps three hours in a hot, noisy train, fitted remarkably smoothly into the invariable routine of the royal day, for unless the Queen was recovering from the recent birth of a child, she never made any concession to the rigours of a journey. If she had made the crossing in the morning, she would go straight into luncheon, and then out in the afternoon with Albert, walking all around the place inspecting the activities and constant

Queen Victoria and Albert Edward, Prince of Wales, by Winterhalter, 1846. The Queen had an uneasy relationship with her heir; on 22 November 1846 her journal records 'he is a very good child and not at all wanting in intellect, but he is awkward, and does not do himself justice.'

On 9 August 1852 Leitch painted Victoria and Albert's departure on a visit to King Leopold. All the British steam fleet anchored in Osborne Bay: the royal yacht, *Victoria and Albert*, its tender, the *Fairy*; and the *Odin, Magicienne, Sampson, Barracouta, Retribution, Black Eagle*, and *Vivid*.

improvements which had been going on in their absence. If the weather was at all hot – and Queen Victoria, who liked nothing better than copious draughts of cold air, had her own definition of temperature – then the Queen and Prince were very likely to be found out on the water again, taking an evening excursion on the *Fairy* before dinner.

Victoria's reaction to being at Osborne again depended on where she had just been. It was 'Oh! so different from the smoke of London',[1] the air 'so fine, and refreshing, one drank it in with joy and gratitude';[2] and of course, the contrast between 'here and "dear" Windsor – like night and day'.[3] But if they had been in Scotland, it was quite another story; how she missed the exhilarating mountain air of the dear Highlands, and her 'enjoyable, independent life there';[4] how flat and restricted the island seemed in comparison – Queen Victoria thrived on wishing things were otherwise.

Victoria and Albert visited Osborne about four times a year. There was usually a spring visit in March or April, a chilly time of year, but Albert's young plantations were already giving walkers a surprising amount of shelter from the wind. The older woods were always full of primroses (the Queen usually had a bunch of them on her desk), violets, and anemones which the children picked by the basketful, and in a mild year the pink, white, and crimson camelias on the terraces would already be out.

The royal family came again in May for the Queen's birthday, the time of bluebells and cuckoos, when the island was in the first flush of spring green, and

The royal yacht,
Victoria and Albert, by the
Hon. C. Flower, 1843,
with Her Majesty aboard.

orchards and hedgerows were white with apple blossom and hawthorn; in the woods going down to the sea the nightingales, which Albert had taught Victoria to listen for, were in full voice, and the air was filled with the scent of gorse. As the Queen sat out on the terrace, surrounded by delights of Albert's devising, she sometimes felt quite dazzled by the crimson rhododendrons and camelias in brilliant sunlight; blowsy peonies were in flower, and the scent of the lilacs mingled with the sweet smell of haymaking nearby. At such times the Queen likened Osborne to 'a lovely sweet nosegay'.[5] The Queen and her children put on their summer clothes; muslin dresses for mother and daughters, cotton 'blouses' for the boys with brown holland, or white, trousers. 'Summer life in this enchanting place,' sighed the Queen, 'which combines the beauties of nature, – of sea and land, – with those of art, – and comfort is really a Paradise and I should be content always to live here.'[6] Her courtiers, however, were less hardy, and complained that: 'Her Majesty plays at the royal game of summer worse than ever – all the windows were open and all the noses were blue at and after dinner last night and today tho' people are shivering the Queen I understand doubts whether it is not too hot to drive to *Freshwater* (as if the water would be anything else this weather).'[7]

The third and longest visit of the year began in the middle of July, a sultry season of heatwaves, harvesting, daily bathes for Albert and the children, long hours under the trees in the garden for the Queen, and still balmy nights when Victoria could walk upon the terrace with only Albert and the moon for

The six eldest children at Osborne, by the Queen, 10 June 1850. On 23 May she had noted in her journal how happy Vicky, Alice and Affie had been 'picking the numberless wild flowers which enamel the woods and fields'; here, it seems that Alice is decorating Lenchen with them.

company, the air heavy with the mingled scents of honeysuckle, jasmine, roses, and the lemon-scented *Magnolia grandiflora*, trained against the walls of the terrace. The weather would break in spectacular storms, the sea and sky turning inky blue and the Solent whipped up into angry yellow streaks, usually just as Victoria and Albert had decided to go yachting for a few days, or when visitors were expected. At such times, it seemed to the child Vicky, when she looked out of the nursery window and saw the opposite coast for a moment, very near and dark through the rain, as though England had 'swum up close' to Osborne.[8] For all its solid construction, the house was a noisy place in a storm; the windows 'dimmed and chattering', the wind moaned around outside corners and in at keyholes, curtains stirred, lamps and candles flickered, chimneys howled and doors banged. The children were confined to the house and galloped up and down the long corridors, and the royal couple battled out with umbrellas and waterproofs.

For some weeks at the end of August, Victoria and Albert would go to Balmoral, the Scottish estate which Albert began to 'improve' and rebuild as soon as the major works at Osborne were finished. They left behind a tearful nursery of the youngest children at Osborne. All returned to the Isle of Wight for a short visit just before Christmas (Albert never spent a Christmas there), when a north-easterly wind off the sea could set against the terrace-front and penetrate to the bone, annihilating any tepid gusts issuing from the decorative

grilles of Cubitt's heating apparatus in the corridors, and even the Queen admitted it was cold. When Beatrice was asked what windows were for she replied unhesitatingly 'To let in *wind*', a *bon mot* pounced upon and feelingly passed on by the Queen's ladies-in-waiting. 'Osborne is *not* a winter residence', wrote one long-suffering tutor; 'Everything is calculated for summer enjoyment. How bleak the terraces now look. Those pretty vases, which one cannot help associating with geraniums and other bright-coloured garden gems, are standing in their damp nakedness almost an eyesore, on the moist terrace.'[9] Nevertheless, Osborne was generally mild and fresh after Windsor, and the sitting rooms were fragrant with large bouquets of chrysanthemums, aromatic myrtle, spears of veronica, sweetly-scented daphnes and Malmaison roses – all raised in the open air.

Victoria and Albert's day at Osborne began at about seven, when the wardrobe maid came in to open the shutters on the tall bedroom windows which overlooked the terrace. 'Splendid sunshine on waking, the room so bright and light, so different from London', the Queen would later remark.[10] Albert usually got up then, pulling on his long white drawers with the feet made in one, the slippers embroidered by his wife and daughters, and his quilted dressing gown, and went to his study–dressing room for what he called the 'golden morning hour'.[11] In summer, the morning sun came slanting in through the windows; in winter a fire burned in the little grate, and he worked

The pergola on the lower terrace, by W. L. Leitch. In her journal for 18 July 1854 the Queen wrote: 'We breakfasted on the terrace, with its fountains playing and the air perfumed with the smell of orange blossoms, and roses, which quite cover the pergola.'

Prince Albert, photograph by William Kilburn, 1848. Photography was in its infancy; the Prince, as ever, was fascinated by the newest technology.

by the light of a green German lamp, a copy of the original which he had brought with him from Coburg. Overlooked by the saints and Madonnas of his Italian masters, he would begin his endless letters and memoranda.

Even at Osborne, Albert had to start his day early if he was to get through the relentless agenda that he had set himself. The Queen did not have a private secretary; this role was filled by Albert, and as in every other area of their lives together – in the running of her establishments, in the upbringing of their children, in emotional support – she completely relied on him. He drafted, clarified, advised, and she approved nothing that he did not agree with. This self-imposed task of supporting, and moulding, a constitutional monarch, who also made considerable emotional demands on him, would have been burden enough for most men. But for Albert, it was only part of his work, for the German Prince had taken on an active role in the cultural life of his adoptive country. There are today many institutions, taken for granted as pillars of the establishment, which owe their existence, or their appearance, in part to Albert. He is regarded as the architect of the modern monarchy; and when his great-great granddaughter, Queen Elizabeth II, waves to the people from Buckingham Palace, she does so standing on the balcony which was Albert's idea. Of all his achievements, he is perhaps best known for the Great Exhibition of 1851, that quintessentially Victorian union of art and technology, but this was only one of a long series of projects. In the realm of arts, for instance, he was Chairman of the Royal Commission that was set up to redecorate the Palace of Westminster; he encouraged the avant-garde purchase of some of the paintings which today are among the National Gallery's proudest exhibits; and throughout the country he encouraged the great provincial galleries which made art accessible to the people. He designed palaces, cottages, farm-buildings, jewellery for his wife and daughters, and instigated pioneering art-historical projects in the arrangement and cataloguing of the Royal Collection. As Chancellor of the University of Cambridge he was no mere figurehead, and achieved considerable reforms in the curriculum. He came to be seen by men of science as the champion of progress. The overwhelming business of administering these wide and active interests went on at Osborne as it did in Windsor or London; though perhaps here was less exhausting, as he was not constantly fatigued with the uncongenial strains of city life.

The Queen, in contrast, would not rise until about eight when Albert would return and give her his English letters to look through for his rare mistakes. If she was already up and in her dressing room, she would hear the bedroom door open and close again, and he would follow her into her dressing room to ask her a name or a date or a spelling. Usually the Prince was ready before the Queen, even though she took the shortcut in the morning of having her maids simply twist her hair, having it 'made' as she called it, later.[12] The youngest child was usually brought down to her while she dressed. Albert would wait for them in the sitting room next door, seated at his desk, which stood side by side with the Queen's, and where there were two more of the green German lamps, and would begin reading some of the endless despatches which the Queen had passed over to 'H.R.H's side' for him to see. If the Queen was ready first, she and the child would go through to Albert's dressing room where he could be heard laughing and talking with Cart, the Swiss valet, who had been with him since he was seven and who seemed 'quite part of himself'.[13] There was Albert, already shaved, perhaps putting on his trousers, which he always wore strapped under the instep and which made him look so 'nice and gentlemanlike' in the Queen's eyes, and which the four-year-old Beatrice particularly loved to see him put on; if she was too late she would say 'What a pity'. He would stand in front of the large looking glass over the chimneypiece and adjust the blue ribbon of the Order of the Garter which he always wore, fasten his waistcoat over it and they were off down the stairs to breakfast, father and child hand in hand.

In the summer, whenever it was fine, they breakfasted outside, naturally, with such children as were old enough to be persuaded to behave. It must have been delightful on the terrace 'with its fountains playing and the air perfumed with the smell of orange blossoms, and roses, which quite cover the pergola'.[14] The Queen, perhaps, would be dressed as she was seen one day in the garden,

The royal couple, photograph by William Kilburn, 1854. Keeping still for the camera always froze the Queen's expressive, lively face into disapproving immobility.

OPPOSITE: One of the greatest pleasures of Osborne for the Queen were the long walks that she and Albert could take there together.

Queen Victoria's sitting room, photograph by Jabez Hughes, 1875.

The family, in this case Prince Albert to the Duchess of Gloucester, wrote to one another on paper headed with vignettes of Osborne.

'very smart in a white gown with flounces and a yellow silk mantalet, covered with lace'; and Albert informal in a coat 'the colour of curl papers', and trousers the colour of whitey-brown paper with the famous off-white 'Albert boots', which had little black tips. Out in the sun he wore a straw hat. When they were seated at the breakfast table, Victoria and Albert each had in front of them a pot of coffee kept hot over a lamp, with milk and cream jugs beside, filled, no doubt, with the ample produce of the Alderney cows at Barton. The Prince's breakfast consisted of an egg, a roll and butter – his Gentlemen, in the Household dining room, were more likely to be tucking into beefsteak and prawns. The Queen's loud laugh would ring out as Albert, dipping his sweet German bread in his coffee, told funny anecdotes about his boyhood at Coburg, or the doings of the Highlanders at Balmoral. Here at Osborne there were no newspapers at breakfast for him to bury himself in as he did at Windsor and Balmoral; they were fetched from the mainland later in the morning, providing the weather allowed. The alcove on the lower terrace became a favourite outdoor spot, though, in late summer, the royal breakfasters were inclined to be tormented, sometimes beyond endurance, by wasps.

After breakfast the Queen took her morning walk, never happier than when she could follow Albert about while he gave directions for improvements. She would then establish herself in some shady part of the grounds – it would never do to become sunburnt – under the trees or in the alcove, where she would sit for the rest of the morning, with a dachshund or two close by, writing letters and working at the relentless flow of papers in the red despatch boxes. Osborne may have been quiet and secluded, but for the sovereign and her consort it was

Alice under the trees with
Helen of Albany reading Books.
July 10 - 1852.

Both asleep.

Aly dd: Oct: 1848
V.C. —

A day-to-day sight at Osborne, the Queen with her Ladies and a child at her knee; photograph by Dr E. Becker, 21 August 1854. From left to right: the Hon. Flora McDonald, Queen Victoria, Arthur, and the Marchioness of Ely.

business much as usual, though with fewer social obligations than London, they had more time for their country occupations. From time to time the Queen held a Council, at one o'clock in the Council Room; otherwise, this was the time of day when, in the summer, Albert would swim, and the Queen would spend half an hour or so before luncheon painting and sketching.

Luncheon was usually taken at two o'clock sometimes, during a heatwave, outside – with the children, Albert dishing out his 'dear reprimands' when they sat badly or forgot their table manners.[15] In his later, overworked years, he would come running in late, his hands full of papers and his face 'full of occupation', and read through half the meal, the worried Queen urging him to eat more slowly as he hurried through the light dishes which did not upset his delicate constitution.

There was always another outing late in the afternoon; only the very worst of what the sea winds could hurl up the long slopes of Osborne kept the Queen indoors: 'We went out at four and got caught in a violent snowstorm,' she recorded one winter, 'so that we took shelter in the greenhouse, after which it cleared, and we were able to walk down to the sea. It is so refreshing here.'[16] This afternoon sortie might take the form of another walk, but very often a fine summer evening meant a drive around the neighbouring countryside. The Queen's carriage would arrive at the Queen's entrance under the portico of the Pavilion, the horses fresh, curvetting and impatient to be off; if Her Majesty were delayed, the coachman would keep them on the move round the circular sweep as they waited until the Queen appeared at the door. Sometimes Albert drove her – she felt so safe with him at the reins; sometimes he cantered along

OPPOSITE: In July 1852, Alice sprained her ankle; she was carried outside to lie under the trees, where her governess, Madame Rollande, read to her, and the Queen, working close by, sketched them on a piece of writing paper (*above*). An earlier sketch of Dacko, 1848, shows a similar spontaneity (*below*).

beside her – how she could admire him then! In hot weather, the Queen would escape to the cool of the water, and steam away in the *Fairy* where she presided over the tea table, the tablecloth lashed to the legs, but otherwise all the fine silver teapots and grandeur just as if they were at home. Not a moment was wasted; the Queen often sketched from on deck, and Albert seized the opportunity to write letters.

They returned in time to dress for dinner. Evening clothes were *de rigueur*, and accounts of visits to Osborne are riddled with guests unable to dine with the Queen because the baggage containing their evening clothes had failed to

Queen Victoria setting out for carriage exercise, *c*.1857. From left to right: Lenchen, Albert (standing), Alice, the Queen, and Augusta, Hereditary Grand Duchess of Mecklenburg-Strelitz. The other top hat may belong to the Hereditary Grand Duke of Mecklenburg-Strelitz.

arrive. She herself made concessions to her island Trianon by wearing wreaths of natural flowers or ivy in her hair, twining ribbons or diamonds into them on a red-letter day. Every time, Albert was consulted for his opinion. The Queen, on her own admission, never so much as put on a bonnet without asking him what he thought. And when her dressers had put the finishing touches to her coiffure, the Queen could see how she looked in the looking glass that Albert had given her for Christmas in 1853, of blue and white Minton porcelain set about with playful Cupids, with matching porcelain trays and pots, on the table in the window of her dressing room.

One fine evening, while the Queen was finishing her toilette and Lady Lyttelton was upstairs in her room gazing at the sunset, the sound of the Prince playing the organ floated out of his open window. 'Such a modulation!' exclaimed Lady Lyttelton, 'minor and solemn, and ever changing and never ceasing.' She pondered on the enigma that was Albert; polite, charming, reserved, dignified, who never truly let go, or expressed his innermost feelings except at such moments, which contrasted so disquietingly with his practical

OPPOSITE: *Queen Victoria*, by Winterhalter, 1855. When the Queen dressed for dinner at Osborne, she would often wear natural flowers in her hair, adding jewels when guests were present.

exterior. How was it, she wondered, that he was capable of the melancholy strains which came in so exactly as an accompaniment to the sunset, and could then go 'to cut jokes and eat dinner and nobody but the organ knows what is *in him*, except indeed by the look of his eyes sometimes'?[17]

The table was sometimes set *à la russe* with the dessert on the table, with silver candelabra and, if distinguished guests were being entertained, a blue-and-white Minton dessert service, but it was more usual at Osborne for Victoria

The drawing room at Osborne, *c.*1858. It was a room full of colour, with gilded ceiling, yellow damask furnishings, and a carpet specially woven to fit round the pillars. When the shutters were closed, full-length mirrors reflected back the light from the chandeliers and candelabra.

and Albert to dine quietly with some of the ladies and gentlemen of the Household. Victoria and Albert either sat opposite one another, or side by side, Albert on the Queen's left. The Queen and the Ladies withdrew to the drawing room after dinner, and the gentlemen stayed on to discuss politics or science until a page came in with a message from the Queen to ask Albert why he was taking so long.

After dinner came coffee in the drawing room, the Queen seated on a sofa with one of her ladies-in-waiting, and the Duchess of Kent, if she was staying, falling asleep in a chair by the fire. Albert would stand in his favourite position in front of the fire with his back against the chimneypiece and one foot on the fender, sporadically 'frightening up' the old Duchess out of her slumbers.[18] They played innocuous parlour games like Hammer and Clock, and Twenty-

One. The Queen tried her hand at billiards on Albert's Italianate table, but was not really an enthusiast. She learnt whist, played for threepenny points at a large round table, soon deciding that she could manage it 'really very successfully' without any help,[19] but still wary of partnering Albert, who was in a position, as her ladies-in-waiting were not, to scold her 'abominably' when she trumped his best cards. Her Ladies were much relieved when she gave up revoking and trumping her partner's aces, but she could never remember to

'Lebewohl', a melancholy tale of parting, composed by Prince Albert. He was a reserved man, for whom music was an important outlet of self-expression.

return her partner's lead and no one cured her of asking how often each suit had been played and how many trumps were out. If there were very few guests, Albert might take up the cards on his own for a hand of patience, La Belle Luise or La Princesse Héréditaire. Often there was music, particularly if one of the Queen's ladies-in-waiting was at all accomplished, though the piano and their own voices were the more usual instruments of entertainment. A discussion over German and Scots music might end when the Prince 'slipped into the music chair', and the Queen 'pulled out some music books, and they picked out songs and scraps of songs together until she was tired and removed to the round table'.[20] At about a quarter to eleven the Queen retired, and her ladies-in-waiting, so often 'excessively sleepy' after a long day in the sea air, sketching, walking, driving and boating, were free to go to bed.

The Council Room, by James Roberts, 1861. It was used for the routine business of a sovereign, but because of the small size of Osborne doubled as ballroom or theatre on royal birthdays, and a drawing room for formal visits by foreign royalty.

The evenings which the Queen undoubtedly enjoyed most were those when she could close the day's entry in her journal with the simple line, 'dined alone and read and played'. Such evenings found Victoria and Albert upstairs in the Queen's sitting room, occupied with a variety of pursuits. They might have been looking over toys for forthcoming birthdays or for Christmas; but they were just as likely to be examining the latest stage in Albert's pioneering project to have a photographic record of all the known works of Raphael. Or they might be pleasurably engaged over the collection of prints or woodcuts of their journeys which they assembled for pasting into Journey Albums. Similarly, they arranged View Albums of sketches of rooms and places they visited and when photographic *cartes-de-visites* became fashionable, Albert began to make up albums of them too.

After a while the albums were laid aside, and the Queen settled on the sofa, where she read aloud to Albert who sat in the chair next to her. Occasionally he would draw while she read, finishing at about half past ten. Among the novels which they read together were Walter Scott's *The Talisman* which the Queen found 'so interesting and romantic'.[21] Miss Austen entertained and amused the Queen with *Pride and Prejudice* and *Northanger Abbey*, and Alexandre Dumas gave so much enjoyment in *La Tulipe Noire* that the Queen embarked almost immediately upon *La Dame aux Camelias*. The Frenchman, however, was not possessed of Miss Austen's singular gift for pinning down the human condition with unimpeachable propriety; *La Dame aux Camelias* was 'beautifully written and interesting', said Queen Victoria, 'but somewhat improper'.[22] One author alone wove such a potent spell that she kept Victoria and Albert up long past their accustomed hour; after reading Charlotte Brontë's 'melancholy, clever and interesting'[23] tale of *Jane Eyre* the Queen went to bed late, 'quite creepy, from the awful account of what happened the night before the marriage, which was interrupted in the church'.[24] The daughter of the Haworth vicarage again kept Her Majesty out of bed to find out what happened when Jane eventually found Mr Rochester.

Usually, though, these quiet evenings drew to a close with music, and for a while Victoria and Albert sat side by side at the piano playing their favourite pieces together; in particular, Mendelssohn who had composed duets especially for them. Albert was a more exacting performer than Victoria even though he laughed when their fingers were stiff and out of practice; she admired his sight reading, the way he played the bass, and how particular he was about keeping time and observing the expression. Sometimes they sang, the Queen generally accompanying, from one of the two volumes in which all their favourite duets were written out.

When the Queen withdrew to her dressing room preparatory to going to bed, Albert would sometimes follow her, and while her maids began to undress the Queen, he would stand leaning against the fireplace, discussing the evening – if they had had guests – and perhaps commenting on the Queen's toilette, sometimes criticizing her dressers if he thought her dress badly fastened, or that there was something wrong with her jewels; then with a stroke on her cheek, and one of those looks which she loved, or a pat on her shoulders (when they were alone he often told her how pretty he thought they were), he was off to his own dressing room. Sometimes he sat in an armchair and read while he waited for her, though in later years he tended to go to bed first. When the Queen finally joined him, Albert turned out the light which had been burning on his side, and, as the lonely Queen was later to remember, she laid her head on that 'dear bosom', feeling as safe as a rock, and as though 'there was no other world but ourselves'.[25]

The peaceful and secluded daily life of the royal couple at Osborne was sustained by a great number of people. Life at the court of Queen Victoria was a series of magic circles, divided by invisible, inviolate distinctions of rank and class. At the centre were the Queen and Prince; around them were grouped the royal family; beyond them again were the ladies and gentlemen of the Court, who made up the Household: private secretaries, ladies-in-waiting, equerries. Further still from the centre were the governesses and tutors, who suffered under just the same ambiguity of status in the royal establishment as they did

OVERLEAF: In the Council Room hung portraits on Sèvres porcelain of the Queen and Prince Albert. These exquisite copies of original portraits by Winterhalter were presented to the Queen by Louis Philippe, King of France, in 1846.

elsewhere, for although they were ladies and gentlemen they were nevertheless officially classified as servants. Members of the outer groups could only step across the division at the express invitation of someone from an inner group.

In a parallel, and quite separate world, a large number of people worked behind the scenes to keep Queen Victoria, her family, Household and guests comfortable at Osborne. Everyone in this army had a specific role and status in a hierarchy which was every bit as rigid and jealously-guarded as the protocol that dictated the order in which the Queen and her guests went into dinner. At the top of the list were Victoria and Albert's personal servants: her dressers and wardrobe maids, and his valets and Jäger. Then there were the upper servants such as the clerks of the kitchen, the master cooks, the confectioner, the table deckers, and the housekeeper. Lower in the order ranked the lamplighters, ushers, apprentice cooks, footmen, under-butlers and nurserymen.

The kitchen, photographed in the mid-1870s, was situated as far as possible from the Queen's dining room to avoid even the suggestion of a smell of cooking anywhere near the Queen.

They came and went unseen by royalty and Court in the network of service passages and staircases hidden away inside the massive walls of Osborne, unless their duties required them to be visible; like the footmen, 'gorgeous and alarming'[26] in scarlet and gold, with powdered hair and silk stockings, such large men that it was said they were hired by the length, who waited at the door or carried messages round the house. Otherwise, the cavernous basement was the servants' principal domain. It was designed with more thought than was often expended on service areas in big houses, and a subaqueous light penetrated all but the coal vaults. The windows onto the outside of the building were all below ground level, and looked out into the blank walls of the area which ran most of the way round the house. But because the house was built on a slope, the kitchens, at the furthest end from the Pavilion, were at ground level.

Under the Council Room were the wine and beer cellars, the valets' cleaning room, the silver-cleaning room and silver pantry (where two men took care of the silver plate – the Queen's gold service never went to Osborne) and the lamp-cleaning room where three lamplighters attended to the eighty-seven patent lamps, replenishing them from casks and cans on the stands in the oil store across the way. In 1860 Albert took advantage of the new amenity of gas, which was piped from East Cowes to the stables, detached offices and buildings, courtyards and grounds. It might have been modern, but it was inefficient, and even dangerous. On dark winter evenings the Queen's coachman could hardly see to draw up under the portico. The supply fluctuated and burners could suddenly flare up in a way that frightened new servants. This was not the reason for the absence of gas in the main house, however; the truth was far more commanding: 'The Queen', wrote Victoria, 'has a great objection to *gas*, and thinks it causes great smells and is unsafe.'[27]

Under the Main Passage, below Albert's ranks of statues, marched the coal vaults, handy for the voracious appetite of the water-heating apparatus. In the basement of the Household Wing, under the Household dining room, were the coffee room, the footmen's room, the clerk of the kitchen's bedroom, the linen

room, the servants' hall, and the servants' hall scullery. When the telegraph was installed, also in the basement of the Household Wing, so was a telegraph clerk. Even at the quietest of times he was a busy man and a crisis pushed him to the limit; the Crimean War, he said, had nearly killed him. The telegraph kept Osborne in touch with the outside world at remarkable speed. A message sent from the Isle of Wight reached Balmoral, over five hundred miles away, in thirty-three minutes.[28]

The kitchen, the first of Albert's new buildings to come into operation, was separate from the main house, and attached to the Household Wing by a covered way. It was as far as possible from the Queen's dining room, to prevent even the suspicion of a smell of cooking, and incidentally minimized the danger of fire. Stewing ovens, steam kettles and roasting spits dated from the very first, but Albert kept the kitchens up to date, and after 1860 ten gas stoves were installed and the master cooks fell victim to the temperamental supply, complaining for years that they had to 'fly to extemporized measures to prevent the spoiling of the Queen's dinner'.[29]

The kitchens had to cater for huge numbers. In 1850 there were fifty-seven servants in the house; by 1861 the number had increased to eighty-three. Many

Kitchen and offices, photograph by A. Disderi, 1867. The Household Wing is on the left, and beyond it the Main Wing and the clock tower. The buildings were carefully designed so that servants could not overlook their royal mistress.

of them slept in the Italianate servants' dormitory, completed in 1850. Footmen, lamplighters, steward's-room men, assistant table deckers, coal-porters, scourers, roasting cooks and apprentices shared rooms here, where they were taken every night in a wagon, even though it was only a few minutes walk away. The upper servants slept close to their workplaces: Albert's valet slept in His Royal Highness's Wardrobe – a room, not a piece of furniture. Frieda Arnold, a homesick, observant German, who was one of the Queen's dressers in the 1850s, was lucky; she lived close to her mistress in the flagtower, where she had a view of the sea and could always hear the 'delightful splashing' of the fountain down on the terrace.[30] Other upper servants, Albert's Jäger, the master cooks, the confectioner and the messenger, each had single rooms in the basement. The under-butler slept, for reasons of security, in the bed hidden in a cupboard in the silver pantry. One attendant slept in the boot-cleaning room.

Frieda Arnold's working day started at eight; she was woken by a housemaid at seven. Cleaning staff started even earlier. Albert was:

. . . very particular, and didn't like attendants in his rooms after their proper hours; but if *he* interrupted *them* it was always with an apology. And sometimes he would be up and out at six o'clock in the morning, and if any servants were about cleaning passages or stairs it was always 'Don't mind me. I am sorry to trouble you.' And his greeting was always *so* pleasant and he always lowered his hat *so* politely.[31]

Although the servants' duties were lighter at Osborne than in London they did not enjoy being there. Married men and women were cut off from their families and they found the rural idyll dull. Free time was rare, precious and uncertain. Frieda Arnold and her colleague Sophie Weiss suddenly heard that the Queen might be going away for a whole day, and taking only one of the wardrobe maids. 'What luck!', exclaimed Frieda:

Before our mistress said anything to us herself, which did not happen until shortly before the said day, good Sophie and I hovered in constant fear and hope as to whether it was true or not. It is so ridiculous, and now I speak of it I cannot help laughing, what great value a single day can have: the very air one breathes seems to change at the thought of being *free*, one almost believes one has wings; never in my life have I walked so lightly as on that day – I never felt tired, and I was full of . . . such happiness.[32]

When the Queen left Osborne after a visit, she took many of the servants with her, but besides those who ministered directly to the creature comforts of Queen and Court, there were others who stayed behind, responsible for the maintenance of the house. The housekeeper, of course, remained there permanently. Elizabeth Smith, who held the position from 1856 until 1887, at a salary of £112 a year and £75 'board wages', enjoyed the advantages of a sitting room 'elegantly furnished', with windows looking onto the gardens and the sea, but felt 'a very heavy responsibility and while she had only superintendence it was a weighty matter'.[33] Some housemaids, such as the two who looked after the Queen's rooms while she was away, were also permanent, but the housekeeper also relied on casual labour, and before the Court arrived, would draft in extra charwomen from the estate and send for extra housemaids from Windsor, to get the place ready. Thus, the work of many hands not only went into sustaining the Queen during her visit, but also into preparing

Osborne for it, so that on arriving from Windsor, she could note: 'The house, as usual, most comfortable.'[34]

Visitors to Osborne were struck by the care and attention to every detail; even the doorscrapers and brushes, where muddy boots could be scraped off, had wooden covers placed over them at night to protect them. Doors swung silently; thick carpets hushed every footfall; the rooms were comfortable and thoughtfully provided with everything a guest might need. The portfolio on the writing table was always kept full of headed writing paper and the inkstand replenished. In winter a fire blazed in the grate. The fine bedlinen was marked with the crown and 'VR' underneath in red needlework, and for the washstand there were plenty of towels which even if only used once were whisked away and replaced. Albert had not only created a home for his wife and family, but an atmosphere which struck any visitor: 'How different *Osborne* is to a *public*, *national* home of royalty!' wrote one, 'It is like going to a *private home*, grand as it is, and fenced off by natural and needful barriers like any large establishment – still it makes you feel it is *private*, and that you are for the time of its belonging and permitted numbers and entrance.'[35]

Osborne from the sea, by Eleanor Stanley, July 1852. This was the view, one of their last sights of England, that Queen Victoria's subjects would see as they sailed from Southampton for the furthest corners of her empire.

85

CHAPTER FOUR

LIFE IN THE ROYAL NURSERY

As Osborne grew, so did the royal nursery. Queen Victoria gave birth to her first child, Victoria, the Princess Royal, on 21 November 1840. Vicky, as the child was always called, did not remain alone in the royal nursery for very long. Twelve days before her first birthday she was joined by a brother, Albert Edward, Prince of Wales, known to his family as Bertie. Seventeen months later came Alice on 25 April 1843, and then Alfred, or Affie, on 6 August 1844. It was at this point, when they had four children, that Victoria and Albert bought Osborne and Albert initiated his 'improvements'. It was just as well that the young father provided such unusually well thought-out and spacious accommodation for his children, for his wife went on to present him with another five pledges of her affection: Helena who was always known in the family as Lenchen, was born in 1846; Louise in 1848; Arthur in 1850; Leopold in 1853; and Beatrice in 1857. Of course, with their births spread out over seventeen years, the children were not all in the nursery at the same time; before Arthur and Leopold were born their older brothers had already been separated from their sisters and the nursery governesses and had been put into the charge of tutors. And while nursery staff were busy making ready the little dresses of muslin and lace for the arrival of the last baby, the expectant Queen was ordering a trousseau for Vicky.

In 1845, however, worries over trousseaux and husbands were far in the future. When the Queen and Prince visited the house in March they took four-year-old Vicky with them. Naturally, the first thing they did was to walk down to the beach, where the Queen fondly watched her daughter's 'raptures' over sand and seashells. That night, Vicky found herself sleeping on a sofa because her bed had not arrived; these were still early days, and the journey to the Isle of Wight had not yet become the well-oiled operation of later years.

The Prince of Wales, by Winterhalter, 1846, in the sailor suit which he first wore that year, and which was the Queen's idea. It set the fashion for small boys for the rest of the century.

Six weeks later they were back again, and this time Vicky had her brother to play with. Bertie had never been to sea before; the ships and the salutes delighted him and he raced wildly about the deck of the royal yacht. The sea air sharpened the children's appetites; they ate a 'famous' supper, and their mother saw them safely to bed. For the next few days they played on the shore and flourished, and when the Queen returned to London she realized how much better they looked than the two babies who had been left behind at Buckingham Palace. So when Victoria and Albert went to Osborne in June, all their children, and the governesses, went with them. On the crossing from Gosport all the children behaved admirably and Alice, noted the Queen approvingly, 'never minded the salutes at all'.[1]

In the pleasure grounds of old Osborne a summerhouse and a tent provided 'charming shade' for the children's games; and another shady tent

The Queen and Vicky, photograph attributed to Henry Collen, *c*.1844–5.

had been pitched on the shore where a cool sea breeze blew. Victoria and Albert breakfasted out of doors in their pleasure grounds with their children playing round them. The Queen was delighted with the green and pleasant scenery of the Isle of Wight, with its 'peeps of the blue sea'[2] and its clear air. She decided that her children looked like roses and that Osborne agreed very well with them. It was a family laying down the foundations of a life at Osborne.

By the standards of their day and rank, Victoria and Albert spent a lot of time with their young family, whether at Windsor, Osborne, or, later on, at Balmoral. When there were no visitors, the children were often at breakfast and luncheon. Albert would sit at the top of the table with, sometimes, a child between him and the Queen. Albert kept them all in order, if they sat badly or untidily, telling his children to eat elegantly, and not to take such big bites. After these meals there was often a game with Papa and one or two children almost always accompanied the Queen on her twice-daily walks and rides. In the evenings when she was 'not much occupied' they would be brought in one or two at a time to play in her room, and she would sometimes go up to the nurseries to see them in their baths and hear their prayers, or creep softly into the nursery after dinner to gaze at them sleeping peaceably in their beds.

The day-to-day care, however, of four, and soon to be five, high-spirited and noisy children, was at this time the formidable task of Lady Lyttelton. She was a kindly woman in her fifties, who had been one of the Queen's ladies-in-waiting. She was tolerant, old-fashioned, and had always felt that she had a vocation as a teacher. Under Albert's directions, she ran the nurseries with strict efficiency. She handled all the accounts, and sent the Prince quarterly résumés of the expenses incurred for each child. She treated them with understanding and affection, though sorely tried by Vicky's tantrums, and

A drawing by the Queen of her four eldest children in July 1846, with the Osborne flag tower in the background.

Bertie's 'tearing high spirits'. It fell to Lady Lyttelton, or Laddle, as Vicky had simplified the unpronounceable syllables of her name, to organize the nursemaids, the wet nurses – Queen Victoria had neither the time nor the inclination to breastfeed her own babies – the children's wardrobes, toys, and their earliest lessons, before governesses took over the girls, and the boys went off to tutors at the age of seven.

Besides the novelty of playing on the shore, where they could be found almost every day, their first summer at Osborne held many treats for the children. They were not yet inured to pomp; it was still fun to kneel at an open window and listen to the band playing outside in honour of a king who had come to luncheon; it was still more fun to go down to the kitchen garden with their parents and gather gooseberries, raspberries, and currants 'to their hearts' content'. There were romps with their father after breakfast, when he would

Affie, Helena (who was always known as Lenchen) and Alice, by Winterhalter, 1847.

wrap the littlest ones in a napkin and swing them backwards and forwards between his legs; or after lunch, when he might paint with the two eldest children; 'such a playful kind darling young father there never was', said Albert's wife.[3] The children's nursery was stocked with lead soldiers, with dolls and tea sets, and there were three sets of spades, rakes and hoes, and three little carts, each with a ladder, basket and shovel. As well as the weighty lesson books bought for the royal children, they also had books of Nursery Tales and Nursery Songs, the stories of Reynard the Fox, Beauty and the Beast, and Robin Hood.

The family idyll was interrupted when three sad faces watched their parents leave for a month-long visit to Papa's boyhood home in Germany. Lady Lyttelton sent the Queen daily bulletins of life in the nursery, and expressed the children's feelings as much as her own when she wrote 'I should fear to be impertinent, if I was to express how very much I feel Your Majesty's and His Royal Highness's absence, which seems to be so much life taken away from us.'[4]

Her letters flew from Osborne to Coburg sparkling with news of the children, and with a catalogue of teeth cut, teething rashes (when Prince Alfred's gums became very hot and full, they were lanced), 'little doses' of rhubarb and milk of magnesia, and diet: how much chicken or mutton, or broth with bread, rice, or vermicelli, had been taken; because the children didn't like puddings, might Lady Lyttelton be permitted to try the addition of some fruit juice? From Lady Lyttelton's letters the parents knew how long the children had spent on the beach that day, and how the Prince of Wales had been troublesome at first, but good humour soon returned after 'a good deal of hard digging and ranging about in freedom.'[5] They knew what a pretty picture Prince Alfred had made

Lenchen, by the Queen, 1847. On 12 June 1848 the Queen wrote in her journal: 'it is impossible to see a prettier child, with her large blue eyes, pink cheeks, golden hair, and white skin. Her features and expression are so pretty. She is such a mild, lively little child.'

as he slept on the afternoon's drive, his face on the lap of Mrs Thurston, the nurse; how the Princess Royal had taken to her cold bath; and that Beauty the pony had resolutely refused to carry the panniers in which the royal infants rode, so his duties had been taken over by Donald. They learnt that the children had 'contrived to sleep on till 7 o'clock, in spite of the very noisy hammering of the builders close to their windows, which had begun very actively at 5.'[6]

The parents also knew when things were going wrong, for Lady Lyttelton kept them abreast of the falsehoods and naughtinesses and the punishments she had meted out, some of which seem unduly harsh today. They were apprised of the Princess Royal's altercation over a pink bonnet, which she wanted to walk out in after supper, an argument which ended in the child being 'imprisoned with tied hands, and very seriously admonished and I trust aware of her fault in the right way'.[7] They heard how she had become disastrously overexcited at the end of Albert's birthday, celebrated in his absence, and 'fell into a transport of rage on perceiving that the day was nearly over, and shrieked and roared in the open carriage, for no other reason, luckily in a lonely part of the road.'[8] On another occasion, a similar offence resulted in a 'whipping' for Alice.[9]

When Victoria and Albert came home again they were welcomed at the door by children who had flourished in their absence; Vicky had begun to read German, Bertie had lost his stammer, Alice was speaking more distinctly than she used to, and Affie was walking and had 'become an enormous fellow'. Osborne was agreeing with them.

That winter, there were days when it was mild enough for the children to play out on the beach, and in March 1846 the Queen first drove out in one of

Lenchen, Affie, and Alice, drawn by the Queen at Osborne in 1847. On 2 December she noted in her journal: 'The children come regularly to me of an evening, beginning at 6 with Lenchen, then Affie, Alice, and at 7 the two eldest.'

the new carriages, 'made here, on purpose for us', which were just like one that Albert's brother Ernest had driven at the Rosenau. The Queen sat in front with Lady Lyttelton, with Alice between them, and on the 'sort of box' behind sat Vicky and Bertie, with Affie on Mrs Thurston's lap. The next afternoon found the Queen outside with Albert, who was at his normal winter occupation of planting trees; all four children planted trees, the three eldest 'quite enjoying it and running about and amusing themselves by putting handfuls of mould on their trees'.[10]

The royal family left Osborne in March with four children, and returned in June with five; little Lenchen made the journey a few weeks after she was born, with her wet nurse, an Irishwoman called Mrs Bray, among the nursery staff. A change of scenery did not mean a change in routine, and in the schoolroom, it was business as usual. Bertie, now four and a half, took his first German lesson, but it was Vicky to whom the Queen paid special attention. She was already giving the little girl her weekly religious lesson, and would occasionally hear her other lessons, in French, English history and reading. She began to take Vicky driving with her, the child sitting up next to her mother 'like une grande dame', and Albert riding along beside the phaeton. Vicky was a bright child, who had inherited her mother's passion and her father's mind and though she had not yet learnt to control her hot temper, she was already showing signs of her considerable intellectual gifts. 'She is such an intelligent, wonderfully clever and engaging child', the Queen wrote proudly, adding as an afterthought, 'though sometimes a little difficult to manage.'[11]

There were concessions to the seaside, but they were taken very seriously indeed. On 30 June a 'great nursery event', as Lady Lyttelton put it, took place, and the Prince of Wales was bathed in the sea for the first time. To us it seems extraordinary that a family which had already spent a whole summer on the beach had not yet bathed, but for the children of Victoria and Albert sea bathing was a rigorous business, not to be taken lightly. Bertie was first, as Lady Lyttelton put it, 'successfully brought by degrees to cold sea-water home baths', and then because there were no bathing machines, or professional 'bathers' to accompany the child into the water, Bertie went down with 'only Papa' to plunge him, and Papa's own valet, Cart, to dress him in the tent afterwards. Bertie was 'extremely good', said the Queen, 'and very proud of his performance'.[12] A fortnight later Vicky's delighted shouts greeted her first immersion, in the care of a bathing woman, though of course Albert had come down too, 'to see that it was properly done'.[13]

It was not all quite this serious; if Papa left his trees and buildings and joined them on an afternoon walk there was every chance of a game of hide and seek with him, 'quite like a boy himself' as he played with them.[14] On long fine evenings the Queen would sit out on the lawn, sometimes until after seven o'clock, with the children round her, playing 'merrily' (Lady Lyttelton would probably have said 'noisily') until their bedtime.

It was a busy summer. Vicky and Bertie accompanied their parents on a visit to Guernsey; just the kind of junketing deplored by the long-suffering Lady Lyttelton, who had to restore order and discipline when her overexcited charges returned. A visit from the Queen Dowager and the Princess of Prussia meant being able to come downstairs smartly dressed and listen to the band. At the beginning of September the partridge season opened; Papa went shooting, and Bertie was allowed to go with him for an hour. There followed another cruise, this time to Jersey and Cornwall, with its concomitant disruptions to nursery life; however, Lady Lyttelton was soon writing that the 'royal return' was well over, and everything was in its place again: 'Bad lessons and good ones, pony rides, luncheon, active hurry-scurrying, all has begun again.'[15]

The children moved into the Pavilion at the same time as their parents; during the evening of 14 September, the Queen went up the staircase above her rooms to see her children 'peacefully asleep in their beds, and so nicely established'.[16] They slept well, and the next morning were all in high spirits and delighted with their new surroundings.

Vicky shone at all she did. Her new governess, Miss Hildyard, who offered

The Queen wrote her journal for 7 December 1847 around her drawing of 'Little Affie playing in my room.' (Later, the picture was carefully cut out of the journal by Princess Beatrice and pasted into her edited version.)

the young mind a more challenging diet than Lady Lyttelton's *Geography by a Lady*, Edgeworth's *Early Lessons*, or *Conversations on Botany*, and who found a ready response in her eager young pupil, was soon full of Vicky's 'extraordinary cleverness', telling the Queen that the child made her forget she was only six and not nine. Bertie, on the other hand, she found 'more backward'. The Queen agreed; she was touched when her son asked her to do his Sunday lesson with him sometimes, he was a good child, said his mother, and 'not at all wanting in intellect', but he was awkward and did not 'do himself justice'.[17]

Mrs Thurston, who worked in the royal nursery for many years, with, from left to right, Bertie, Lenchen, Vicky, Alice (on the ground), Affie, and the baby Louise; photograph by William Kilburn, 22 June 1848.

Her unspoken, perhaps even unconscious, thought was regret that he was not the image of his father. She never accepted the child for himself, always measured him against her ideal, Albert, and naturally the child never matched up to it. It was a damaging mistake which she repeated with her second son.

It was too cold in the winter of 1846–7 for there to be many days on the beach, but there was still plenty for the children to do and see on walks with Mama. The Guernsey cows which had been given to the Queen after her visit there had calved, and there were three doe-eyed offspring to admire at Barton Farm; Papa always needed help with his tree planting, and one Sunday afternoon was spent 'picking up numbers of acorns from the evergreen oak near the door. We ourselves', wrote the Queen, 'put some into pots, in which work the children helped.'[18] Another day the children gathered up the branches which Albert was trimming. Even a cold snap had its compensations, as the

Queen discovered when she and the children went to see Albert's new ice-house being filled with ice, 'quite a curious performance', she thought, as she watched the men breaking the ice above and 'throwing it down through an opening where we went below to see it falling through, like rain.'[19] When it snowed Albert made a snowman while the children walked about with the Queen and her ladies. Indoors, before the Queen dressed for dinner, she would have all four children in her rooms, 'playing at soldiers and marching about';[20] but the usual evening routine at this period was for Vicky and Bertie to take it in turns to have their supper in the Queen's sitting room, then Lenchen, the youngest, was brought down for a quarter of an hour, followed by Alice, and then Affie. And when the youngest children were left behind in London, as they were when Victoria and Albert went to Osborne in May 1847, the Queen missed them 'very much'.

On 10 March 1847, after a game of billiards with her ladies-in-waiting, the Queen was tempted to paint the snow-covered scene that lay outside.

The following July, though, all the children were taken to Osborne and the happy summer occupations began again. 'We breakfasted out of doors and were much amused in watching the children running about and climbing', wrote the Queen.[21] Vicky and Bertie learnt from their father one Sunday morning how to catch butterflies in their butterfly nets, the Queen watching and enjoying their pleasure. It was a picturesque scene, but with a serious purpose. Albert himself had collected natural history specimens as a child; he now wished his offspring to do the same.

The children were growing fast, and the Queen was particularly enjoying her two youngest. Affie, now three, 'so ridiculous and independent', was wearing his older brother's sailor's dress – a notion of the Queen's which set the fashion for small boys for the rest of the century – which had been shortened for him. He looked 'such a darling' in it on his birthday, and 'running about everywhere by himelf' at the rustic fête held in honour of his father's birthday. Little Lenchen showed a touching fondness for her dear Papa, and for his music, holding up a finger when there was something she particularly liked. She would follow him about everywhere, wrote the Queen, a 'dear little rosebud, but rather violent tempered!'[22] When Vicky, Bertie, Alice, and Affie were out with their parents, it seemed like a dream to the Queen: 'I saw my beloved one, looking so young, followed by these four little people. It seems but yesterday that we married, and then again, also much longer.'[23] When the beloved one went partridge shooting in September, they all followed him, seeing 'a good many' birds shot, and the children were very happy, and proud to be allowed to carry home some partridges. In December they helped him plant rhododendrons behind the kitchen gardens, and when it was blowing 'a fearful hurricane outside' with deluges of rain he amused them by playing billiards for them and giving them a magic lantern show.

Alice, now four and a half, was taking her daily reading lesson with the Queen and all the children were coming regularly to her in the evening, beginning at six o'clock with Lenchen, then Affie, Alice, and at seven, the two eldest. Another girl, Louise, was born on 18 March 1848, and made the crossing to the Isle of Wight with all her brothers and sisters when she was only three weeks old. This was the earliest that the Queen would travel after a confinement. The Queen looked into Louise's cradle at Osborne and she regretted that this fine strong baby had not been a boy, in spite of telling herself that it would be very ungrateful to complain, when she herself had come through her confinement so well: the Queen sometimes felt that she had enough good health for both herself and Albert.

From the little carriage, her 'garden chair', pulled by a pony, in which she normally took her exercise in the weeks following childbirth, the Queen watched her children picking the violets, anemones and primroses which 'enamelled' the woods and banks of Osborne. On Maundy Thursday, following the custom which Albert had brought with him from Germany, the children hunted round their parents' breakfast table for the hard-boiled eggs coloured pink, golden, yellow, brown, black and light green, which he had hidden for them. They went to see the sheep being washed and sheared at Barton. While they were out, Lady Lyttelton seized the opportunity of a quiet moment to write home: 'all the children are out with the Queen and Prince, attended by the bailiff, to see the sheep shorn; and to hear the merry distant laugh, and catch glimpses of their little graceful figures dotting round the park, one would think all was happy and promising.'[24]

From the pages of the Queen's journal we might be forgiven for thinking so too, for Queen Victoria has left posterity with glimpses of Osborne during the 1840s as a long family idyll, ruffled, certainly, by occasional awkwardness, but generally her good chicks are as pretty as roses, romping about her as she sits working under the trees in the pleasure ground or in her cosy new sitting room; Alice and Affie are industriously and earnestly repeating their little lessons to her, and when the Queen climbs the stairs under the fresco of Britannia, and passes the statue of Albert she finds Lenchen looking so pretty in her bath, with her large blue eyes, pink cheeks, golden hair, and white skin.

It was the hard-pressed Lady Lyttelton, the French, English, and German governesses, and the nursery staff who coped with the 'roughish' days of 'naughtinesses, blunders, and interruptions'. Lady Lyttelton saw nothing to look forward to 'in the middle of the usual birthday worrets; aggravated by company, and by a sad disgrace of the Prince of Wales's and the prospect of an unmanageable tea-party of fourteen children!'[25] But her fondness for these unruly princelings was undeniable; Affie, whose fourth birthday celebrations were the cause of her outburst, she reported to be 'in great beauty, all blue and silver, bewildered with presents, and much preferring to *all* a penny trumpet given by Princess Royal, bought with her own shilling.'[26] This in spite of the rival attractions of two small silk balloons filled with gas, or the bearskin cap and the sword which Papa had given him.

Moments of quiet were rare enough for Lady Lyttelton to write home about. Even if the children were behaving, their accounts still had to be seen to. Bills, which had to be itemized child by child, came to her for everything from clothes for the wet nurse to the restringing of little pearl necklaces, and the repair of musical boxes and ivory-handled umbrellas covered in best brown silk. She must sort out which of the white lambswool socks and which of the

Receipts for medicine and curling papers bought by the royal nursery, 1847. Lady Lyttelton kept a careful record of the expenses incurred on behalf of each child and every quarter the accounts were presented to Albert.

slate- or straw-coloured kid gloves had been bought for Vicky and which for Alice. She must settle the bills from such as Swan and Edgar for cotton, pins, hooks and eyes, needles, whalebone and silk, for welsh flannel and jaconet muslin. She must check the latest total for the pots of cold cream and the bottles of honey water which were regularly ordered by the royal nursery.

As the children grew, they needed more India rubber waterproof galoshes. As they sat on their Dunstable straw bonnets and their Leghorn chip hats, these had to be re-pressed and repaired. With money from Prince Albert, and keeping a careful record for him, Lady Lyttelton paid the bills for them all: for Affie's twenty-two flannel petticoats; for the dancing master; for Lenchen's eight little pairs of blue, pink, cerise, and straw-coloured quilted shoes, and her

The Osborne nursery, photograph by Jabez Hughes, 1875. Situated directly above the royal apartments, the nursery was light and spacious. Infant mortality was high in Victorian England, but the Queen's robust health contributed to her nine children arriving safely in the world, and Albert's careful management in the nursery helped to ensure that they all lived to adulthood.

scalloped and flounced muslin baby dresses with Valenciennes lace, and embroidered bodies; she paid for the globes and copy books, the quill pens, the lesson books, and the fairy stories; for the dolls and tea sets and lead soldiers, bricks and kites and agate marbles. When Her Majesty came up to the nursery to see her children in the bath, they were being washed with fine sponges and soap of almond milk or peach and their teeth were cleaned with ivory toothbrushes; their hair was brushed with satinwood brushes, and wrapped in curling papers, ordered by the quire, to make tomorrow's ringlets. The cost of it all, down to the ribbons of sky blue satin, peach brocade, or Gordon plaid, the spun silk gaiters, the oiled sponge bags, and packets of violet powder, was accounted for quarterly by Lady Lyttelton to Prince Albert. It was in a rare moment indeed that she could write 'All very peaceful indoors': her accounts were straight, the children good, the governesses 'reconciled' – whether to their pupils or to each other she did not choose to specify – and dear Vicky 'playing a smooth arpeggio in the room beneath this, to crown all'.[27]

There is no doubt that six children under the age of seven and a half were a handful, and Lady Lyttelton must have felt relief as well as a little sadness when in the summer of 1848 Bertie graduated from her nursery jurisdiction to the care of his first tutor, Mr Birch, a mild man of whom the child was fond. Now Lady Lyttelton could watch with a careless eye the Prince 'at high romps' on Albert's new lawns. She envied Mr Birch his hearty, manly voice, which from three storeys up could be heard shouting '*No!* certainly *not!*' and which she felt sure outdid in effect 'many a poor governess's sound reasoning'.[28]

The three eldest children were now bathing every day, Bertie, of course,

separately from his sisters. Every other day, including Sundays, Vicky and Bertie went riding. Bertie was getting bigger and braver, 'so improved in manly ways', having to be checked in a gallop and wanting to run races on rough ground. The noise in the nursery redoubled, as the cousins of the royal children came to stay. Their grandmother, the Duchess of Kent, was greeted on her birthday by nine grandchildren standing in a row in the hall, with nosegays in their hands, such a pretty sight that the Queen sketched it for her diary, a prim little row, but quite unlike the drove of children Lady Lyttelton witnessed being sent indoors by a heavy shower 'shouting, roaring, running and tumbling home, for all the world as if they were cottagers'.[29]

Early in September, Victoria and Albert went to Scotland for a month, leaving Alice, Lenchen, and Louise at Osborne. Even with the Queen away, Lady Lyttelton knew no rest; once, she lost two princesses: 'Yesterday I hunted

The Queen sketched her six eldest children, with their cousins Feo, Ada and Eliza, lined up to greet their grandmother, the Duchess of Kent, on her birthday, 17 August 1848.

all over the house for *ces dames* till I was half dead, and could not think where they were, till I found them both, dressed up in fashionable cloaks and wrapped in patterns of silk and ribbons, in the Queen's wardrobe, where a haberdasher had just brought half his shop.'

They had a chance for some more organized, but less glamorous dressing up in December, when a charade was made up as a surprise for Albert. The Queen spent two afternoons rehearsing it and then sprung it on her husband. She described it in detail in her journal:

The first syllable was 'High' represented by Vicky, Alice, and Alfred in girls clothes, jumping to get some grapes and calling out 'Too high'. The second 'land' Bertie as a sailor came and recited verses and rushed into the arms of his mother and sister, I dressed up as an old woman, and Vicky as a cottage girl. The third syllable 'er' was the scene from 'Frank and Robert' with the little dog Trusty, acted by Bertie and Alice (in Bertie's clothes) with Dandy. The last 'Highlander' a tableau with Bertie, Vicky, Alice, and Lenchen all in kilts, which looked extremely pretty with flags and guns. Albert for whom the whole was a surprise was very pleased. The Highlanders marched about in great glee afterwards. Lenchen who looked wonderful was beside herself with delight and refused to go to bed at all. Vicky made a splendid big boy and looked so tall and masculine.[30]

The charade was such a success that they did another one, which the Queen again enjoyed so much that she gave another full account of the evening's entertainments:

The first part 'Break' represented by Vicky and Alice, who discussed the smelling of some flowers, which Alice finally pulled down, I coming in as an angry grandmother. – 'Fast' the second one was two exhausted children (Vicky and Bertie lying on the ground) and a Lady (I) and her two children (Alice and Alfred) giving them some food and restoring them to life. The last 'Breakfast' represented by the five children at breakfast, Vicky standing on a chair and reciting some verses. Vicky and Alice and Lenchen were dressed as boys and Lenchen also looking too funny in trousers of Alice's, a jacket and cap belonging to the boys – Bertie and Affie quite unrecognizable as girls. Lenchen was delighted and too droll. I invented the whole affair and wrote the dialogue of the two first parts.[31]

'The whole family,' commented one of the Household, 'appear to advantage on birthdays. No tradesman or country squire can keep one with such hearty simple affection and enjoyment.' The royal children who were born in the spring and summer also had birthdays at Osborne: Lenchen's was the day after the Queen's – 'two such merry days and so nice that they follow each other so closely', said the Queen[32] – so she celebrated hers at Osborne too, as did Alice, Affie, Louise, and, occasionally, Arthur, who for a few years shared his with his godfather, the octogenarian Duke of Wellington; the Queen, with her relish for anniversaries always felt that this '*double* birthday was such an interesting one!'[33] A birthday was a red-letter day, when even if the Court was in mourning for one of the Queen's numerous relatives, they sealed their letters that day with red, not black, sealing wax.

Victoria and Albert and their children had a well-established little ceremony on birthdays. At about seven in the morning a band struck up on the terrace outside their windows and when the Queen and Prince had dressed they

The Highland dress, which Louise first wore on 17 December 1849, had originally been worn by Bertie on Albert's birthday in 1843, and later by Affie and Lenchen. The Queen included this sketch in her journal for the day, adding 'Louise looked most absurd, but quite like a little boy.'

would go upstairs to the schoolroom to fetch the birthday child, known as 'The Birthday', who was expectantly waiting for them, and wish him or her joy. Then all three went down to the breakfast room where the rest of the brothers and sisters were assembled and the present table laid out with a wonderful array of toys, books, games, and jewellery. When Vicky was six, she was given 'a fine writing box'. For Alice's fifth birthday (the child 'too pretty, in her low frock and pearl necklace, tripping about and blushing and smiling at all her honours'), her parents gave her jewellery, and the more picturesque than practical present of a live lamb, all decked out with pink ribbons and bells, supposedly tamed by Toward's daughter, but Lady Lyttelton privately considered that its manners were still those of the farmyard. Within a few days her forebodings were borne out, and the lamb had become 'the cause of many tears. He will not take to his mistress, but runs away lustily, and will soon butt her, though she is most coaxy; and said to him in her sweetest tones, after kissing his nose often, "Milly! *dear* Milly! *Do* you like me?"'[34]

When Affie was seven, many of the presents on his table had come from the Great Exhibition. Occasionally there was something worked by the Queen, like the waistcoat which she gave Affie on his tenth birthday. The same year he had two boxes of tin soldiers and a fire engine from Bertie, and a parrot. The presents were not wrapped up, and there were no birthday cards, but usually everyone was wearing new clothes and Albert would be wearing a waistcoat worked for him by Victoria, or his mother-in-law, or one of his daughters. For Louise's first birthday, in 1849, all the girls wore new *mousseline de laine* frocks and the boys new shepherd's plaid kilts, and the Queen had a new dress, both morning and evening.

New Year card from Alice to her father, 1850. The Queen set great store by anniversaries, and her children were encouraged to follow her example.

After the present table there would follow a day of very modest special treats. On Vicky's sixth birthday, at her own particular request, she and Bertie planted trees at Barton with their parents. Each child made the greatest rite of passage at the age of ten or eleven, when Albert took The Birthday out riding. Louise's turn came in 1859, 'alone, her first ride out, in a regular riding habit. It was a treat she herself had begged for.'[35] Perhaps a tree or two would be planted in honour of the day (good practise for later, public, duties). At luncheon the band played again (unless the birthday fell upon a Sunday, in which case it only played in the morning), and if this was a third birthday, the child took luncheon for the first time with its parents, Lenchen looking 'too sweet' with a wreath of ivy leaves in her hair, and in due course, Arthur, 'in a very smart white dress with blue and gold'.[36] At this meal the birthday cake might be cut and the bon bons on it distributed by The Birthday.

Afterwards the children would play some pieces of music for their parents, Affie on the violin which it had been his own idea to learn, and the girls on the

Bertie and Affie catching butterflies, by the Queen, 8 June 1850. Four days earlier, she entered in her journal 'almost too hot to walk, so I sat and wrote under the trees, whilst the boys were running about, catching butterflies, etc.'

OPPOSITE: Lenchen, with her nursemaid Eliza Collins, by Winterhalter, 1850.

piano, becoming competent enough by the time they were about thirteen to manage a Beethoven sonata. In the evening the whole family would gather in the Council Room for an entertainment of some kind. One year there was a conjuror, an elderly Italian called Andreoletti, who deceived and impressed his royal audience with his wonderful sleight of hand. 'There are hardly any preparations', wrote Victoria, 'and he performs all his tricks close up to one, yet without one's being able to make out how they are done.'[37]

Dinner would be accompanied by the band again, and The Birthday, with several brothers and sisters, would 'appear', as the Queen put it, the youngest usually playing the role of court jester, 'in the most tremendous spirits, shouting and laughing',[38] or keeping the whole table laughing with 'droll, inquisitive, and positive remarks'.[39] If The Birthday was a princess, she would be wearing a

The children in the pleasure ground at Osborne, by the Queen, 1850. From left to right: Alice, Affie, Bertie, Lenchen, Vicky, Louise, and Arthur in the arms of Mrs Thurston.

wreath and 'much occupied with her new jewellery'.[40] The youngest stayed until the birthday health was drunk, and then went off to bed. A fourteenth birthday was an occasion for dining with the grown ups for the first time; when it was Lenchen's turn, her mother noted she was looking 'very nice in a white muslin dress, with a wreath of natural flowers in her hair'.[41] As the children grew older, instead of the entertainments in the Council Room, there would be a little dance there after dinner when the Queen might step out in a quadrille with an eight-year-old son, or fondly watch a daughter of seven: 'It was quite touching to see her innocent delight and excitement, mixed with great attempts to make fine steps.'[42] Like the tree-planting, it was all good private practice for necessary accomplishments, and the Queen kept an eye on how her children were shaping up:

Vicky looked extremely well, and danced and held herself very nicely, Alice also, and the boys are much improved in their dancing. After quadrilles, the first of which I danced, walzes, and a reel, the dance concluded with a very merry country dance, in which, however, I did not take part, for fear of tiring myself. It was such a cheery evening, – all ages dancing together, and our dear children all so happy. What could have been pleasanter?[43]

Victoria kept a careful account of the day, as she did every other, in her journal, always prefacing the entry with a little prayer for the safety and well-being of the birthday child, if it was one of the boys praying that he might grow up to become more and more like his perfect father.

'The most important thing that happened', said the thirteen-year-old Prince of Wales when asked to summarize the events of 1853, 'was our beginning our

The Queen on the terrace with her third, and unquestionably favourite, son, Arthur. She gave this painting by Winterhalter to Albert in 1850 and it hung in her sitting room.

The gardens of Albert and his brother Ernest which they had had as children in Coburg, by M. Bruckner. Albert gave each of his own children a plot to work at Osborne, passing on to several of them his passion for the art of gardening.

Swiss Cottage.' This must have seemed a wonderful project to the children. They already had their own gardens at Osborne, whch had been given over to them on the Queen's birthday in 1850, for ever since his children were tiny Albert had tried to foster in them some of his own passion for the art of gardening. In what was then a most unusual and sensitive educational project, but one which seems to us today entirely natural, Albert saw to it that his children were provided with the correct equipment to learn the art of horticulture; there were clogs and garden blouses among the satin shoes and silks and muslins in the princesses' wardrobes, and in the lists of books and toys which the royal nursery regularly purchased from E.C. Spurin of London, Manufacturer and General Repository for Articles of Instruction and Amusement, there was usually another set of scaled-down garden tools, or a painted wheelbarrow, initialled for the latest addition to the nursery in gold at an extra cost of 1s. 6d. They had a tool-house to keep their implements in, with a brick floor which the boys had helped to lay; an orchard had been planted for them; they each had an identical plot, filled with orderly rows: two each of flowers, gooseberries, currants, strawberries and raspberries; and one row each of turnips, beet, onions, carrots, asparagus, peas, beans, parsnips and artichokes. The shrubs nearby had been planted by the four eldest children, with labels on which Bertie had painted the names pencilled out for him by one of the Queen's Ladies.

And now they were to have a real, full-size house of their own. It is likely that the idea was Albert's once again, since it was he who directed the meticulous organization of the nursery and schoolroom. In the grounds of his old home, the Rosenau, was the real Swiss Cottage, complete with outside staircase and cattle downstairs, which the Queen had thought 'so charming' on

The Swiss Cottage in the grounds of the Rosenau, by M. Bruckner. It was a real Swiss chalet and the inspiration for the one built at Osborne. Albert's brother Ernest and his wife stayed at the Rosenau with Victoria and Albert during their visit in 1845.

her visit to Coburg in 1845; and a similar building at Osborne would be an ideal place for the children to gain practical experience in a variety of improving pursuits from museum-keeping to cookery. So on a fine spring afternoon Victoria and Albert and all their children except the baby Leopold drove to the children's gardens, and went through one of the little family ceremonies which Albert so loved to organize. First, Bertie read out a grandiose inscription written on parchment:

The first stone of this Swiss Cottage built facing our gardens was laid by us in the presence of our parents on Ascension day, the fifth of May, A.D. 1853 in the 16th year of the reign of our beloved mother. Victoria Adelaide Mary Louise, Albert Edward, Alice Maud Mary, Alfred Ernest Albert, Helena Augusta Victoria, Louise Caroline Alberta, Arthur William Patrick Albert

The parchment and some coins were put in a bottle which was deposited in the

The Swiss Cottage in the grounds of Osborne, by W. L. Leitch, 1855, built specially for the children, where they could learn to cook and garden. Note the two small boys at work in the foreground.

stonework and the first stone was laid, each of the seven children, down to the three-year-old Arthur, putting on some mortar and striking the stone with a small hammer. All the children, said the Queen, were 'greatly excited and delighted', Arthur in particular being 'great fun'; it must have been a noisy occasion.

The building was to rest on a stone plinth. The two eldest boys helped at the masonry, being paid wages by Albert; 'Affie worked as hard and steadily as a regular labourer', said his mother approvingly.[44] The cottage itself was assembled from ready-made wooden sections, incidentally making it one of the first prefabricated buildings in England. Nevertheless progress was slow, but by November it was finally up and looking, said the Queen, 'so real, that one would fancy oneself suddenly transported to another country'.[45] In every detail it was an authentic Swiss chalet, with wide overhanging eaves, a carved wooden balcony running all round the first floor, rough-hewn boulders holding down the roof, and quotations in German from Psalms and Proverbs on the gables. It really was extremely pretty, thought the Queen, though it was a pity the wood had been coloured and stained rather too dark. On her birthday in 1854 all the family drove down to the children's new domain and it was formally opened and the key to the place that was to become the heart of all that was happiest for them at Osborne was handed over to them.

Unlike the Swiss Cottage at the Rosenau there were no cattle downstairs; instead there was accommodation for a caretaker, Mr Warne, and his wife. There was also a miniature kitchen, with floors and walls of porcelain tiles, a charcoal-burning kitchen range, and a comprehensive *batterie de cuisine*. In the summer of 1854 the Privy Purse settled bills to the value of £75. 13s. 11d. for household goods as this kitchen was equipped. From Bennington and Son in

The kitchen at the Swiss Cottage, photograph by A. Disderi, 1867. Cookery lessons became a real treat for the royal children.

Jermyn Street, London, came the showier articles like the best copper stewpans, saucepans, ornamental pie moulds and jelly moulds (these latter very expensive items at £3. 10s. each), which were arranged in shining ranks along the stout shelves of the dresser in the porcelain kitchen – where they remain to this day – and an armoury of meat choppers and saws, root knives, fancy cutters and French mincing knives. William J. Burton of Oxford Street, London, sent such necessities as goffering and wafer irons, ivory-handled table knives, cake shapes and paste jaggers, as well as the humbler items like the iron serving spoons, wooden pastry board, and enamel pots and pans. Garrards supplied eighteen plain silver dessert spoons and six table spoons and a bill for £17. 5s.

Upstairs, which was reached by an outside staircase, there was a small dressing room with couches and toilet articles; a dining room with chairs, tables, and walls all of carved wood, and a piano supported by carved figures. There was also a room with eight glass cases in it. These were for the children's

Vicky, Bertie, Alice and Affie, with their butterfly nets and collecting boxes; photograph by Dr E. Becker, August 1853. The children were encouraged to collect specimens for their natural history collections in the Swiss Cottage museum.

burgeoning collections of shells, stones, beetles, butterflies, moss and flowers; 'We went to the children's garden,' wrote the Queen, 'where they were extremely happy unpacking all their things for the Swiss Cottage.'[46]

The glass cases in the museum began to fill up with the spoils of the brothers' travels. Affie began relatively modestly with stones and minerals brought back from his visit to Coburg in 1857; later voyages yielded rich harvests of curiosities. Bertie, too, beginning the travels which were intended to broaden his education (though not perhaps in the fields or direction he himself would have preferred) brought back, among other things, rarities from the Micmac tribe of North American Indians. The museum increased greatly, to such an extent that Albert began to plan a new building to house it all. Collecting for the museum was not limited to the royal children; there were other contributors. Lady Canning, for instance, wife of the Viceroy of India and an erstwhile lady-in-waiting to the Queen, sent a collection of centipedes, tarantulas, scorpions, preying mantis, and stick insects. Over the years, a small menagerie grew up at the Swiss Cottage, anything from live lizards and frogs to

Affie (left) and Bertie with their tutor Mr Gibbs, photograph by Roger Fenton, 1854. When the Princes were about seven, they left the nursery, and began to be educated separately from their sisters.

the chihuahua which had been brought to the Queen from Mexico; 'a curious, tiny little dog', she recorded, 'something like a diminutive Italian greyhound.'[47] There was also a donkey which provided great amusement.

The Swiss Cottage rapidly became a central part of the children's life, their 'very favourite spot'.[48] They looked forward to coming to Osborne, and immediately they reached the island they would hurry over to the Swiss Cottage to see how it had all been doing in their absence, how their gardens were getting on, and whether the squirrels had left them any gooseberries or strawberries. Everything else had to wait. Bertie, after he became king, once said that his chosen profession would have been that of a landscape gardener.

Albert soon had the Swiss Cottage and the gardens round it planted with evergreens; and on the Queen's birthday in 1855 she and the six eldest children planted trees there. It became a sheltered place bright with cottage flowers such as hollyhocks. The Queen would often call in on her daily walks and drives and invariably find the children playing or working in their gardens. Occasionally, tempted by such an enjoyable spot, she would stay for a while and write.

As often as not Queen Victoria found her children assembled for a tea or supper that included simple dishes, like pancakes, wafers, and Schneemilch, which her daughters had made themselves; for cooking in the porcelain kitchen had become a regular and popular occupation. Sometimes these teas were honoured by the presence of Mama and Papa, and Albert was obliged to eat the uncertain consequences of his educational experiment; 'I am afraid you don't think our cooking very famous', Alice once admitted to him.[49] He was actually known to have turned his hand himself to a German dish for the children.[50] Invitations were sometimes extended to the children of General Grey, who had

Family group on the terrace, photographed by Dr. E. Becker on the Queen's birthday, 1854. From left to right: Bertie, Vicky, Arthur, Alice, Albert, the Queen, Louise, the Duchess of Kent, Lenchen, Affie. The two dogs, Dandie and Deckel, are in front.

succeeded George Anson as Albert's Private Secretary. One of these was an exact contemporary of Arthur; just like any other proud mother, Her Majesty had observed that 'the baby is large, but not nearly so plump as ours'.[51]

At about the same time as the children laid the foundation stone of the Swiss Cottage, Albert embarked on another elaborate educational project. He consulted Captain Alfred Balliston of the royal yacht and together they planned the construction of a floating bath,[52] in which the children could learn to swim in safety. It was a cumbersome, unseaworthy affair, a cross between a boat and a sieve, which did not ride the water well and the masts from two old line-of-battle ships were moored in place as breakwaters. The hull was painted a tasteful dark blue and the decks were stone-coloured. It had a floor in the form of a wooden grating, rounded off so as to prevent any danger of splinters, which could be raised or lowered according to the age and ability of the swimmers, who were safe within its netting sides, and screened from public view by awnings round the surrounding platform. It had a dressing room that was comfortably furnished with seats and windows, a water closet, a wash-stand with mahogany fittings, and a cistern full of fresh water. The total initial cost was £525. 14s. 6d. Royal bathers were rowed out to it and could swim at any

Bertie, Vicky, Alice, the Queen and Affie, photograph by Roger Fenton, 1854. The four eldest children formed a close-knit group and felt quite 'lopsided' without one another.

stage of the tide – Albert set the work in hand not long after the Queen drove down to the beach intending to bathe, but could not because the tide was too far out to use the bathing machine. Albert's caution was not misplaced; over the years of royal occupation of Osborne several people were drowned there.

The floating bath was launched in 1854 and served its purpose well. On 1 August the Prince of Wales had his first swimming lesson from an Eton waterman named Talbot. Affie had his first lesson on 16 August. Two days later Bertie swam six strokes on his own and was soon proudly announcing that he could swim two breadths of the bath; when he could swim seven lengths, Talbot gave him a prize of a pencil case. Albert's thoughtful, careful mind foresaw the worst and his sons were prepared for it – they even practised swimming with all their clothes on: shirt, drawers, socks, trousers, and boots. The royal family bathed and swam during the summer visit, Albert occasionally bathing with his sons, and during the winter the floating bath was hauled ashore and housed in the shed which was built for it in 1857. It was carefully maintained, and every spring Captain Balliston saw to it that it was repaired and repainted.

A daily swim was in keeping with traditions which demanded athletic prowess in princes but it was more unusual, though typically practical, of

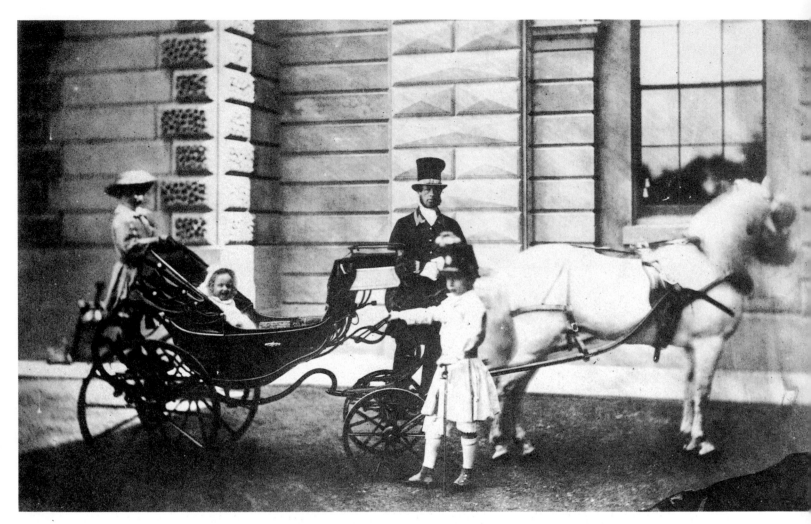

Carriage exercise for Beatrice, drawn by the pony Alderney, with Leopold and Arthur (standing); photograph by Captain Hon. D. de Ros, July 1858.

Undated sketch of a royal infant being carried in a pannier, by Landseer: an alternative to carriage exercise before the children learnt to ride.

Albert to ensure that his daughters also learnt. They were taught by women brought over for the purpose from Boulogne. Vicky took her first strokes in August 1856 under the tutelage of Eugénie Lohy and after Vicky had had a fortnight's lessons, the Queen walked down to the beach and was rowed out to the swimming bath to see that Vicky 'really swims quite nicely now'. When the Queen next wrote one of her regular letters to Vicky's future mother-in-law, she took care to mention that her daughter had now mastered this 'useful' new accomplishment. In 1857 Alice joined Vicky, bathing and swimming super-vised by Isabelle, also from Boulogne. Bertie and Affie bathed daily, of course separately from their sisters, and the younger ones every other day, including Sundays.[53] 'We had such a pleasant bathe yesterday notwithstanding the sea not being very smooth,' wrote Alice to her absent father, 'I swam twice the length of the swimming bath without stopping and I dived several times. I can swim under water quite well and remain under for some time.'[54] Lenchen learned to dive well enough to be able to pick up objects on the bottom.

The strongest presence at Osborne was Albert. On the very rare occasions that he was away from home the children wrote him dutiful but loving letters on the paper headed with charming vignettes of Osborne: 'My dear Papa, Osborne is so lonely without you and we are counting the days till you come back...';[55] 'My dear Papa How long it seems that you are away, I long very much to see you again';[56] 'we miss you all very much it feels so funny without you'.[57] The older children knew what was expected of them but Leopold was only four and his sense of filial loneliness was eclipsed by the irritating habits of his little sister Beatrice: 'Dear Papa I am so unhappy because you are not here Baby makes such a noise and when I am sitting opposite to Baby on the left side of the carriage, she kicks me and she goes on saying *oogly oogly*.'[58]

In such a large family the brothers and sisters fell into natural groups, the four eldest, Vicky, Bertie, Affie and Alice, forming one, seldom separated and never for more than a few days at a time. Parting, when it came, was early and painful – Bertie and Affie felt 'lopsided' without one another.[59] At twelve or thirteen the boys were pushed out into the world, Bertie the better to concentrate on the dreary, intense education so manifestly unsuited to his ability and temperament, and Affie to begin his naval training.

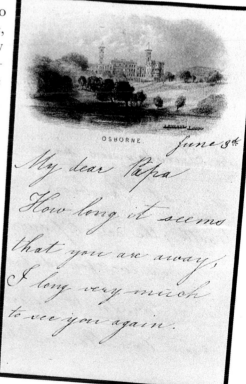

Letter from Louise (aged ten) to her father, 1858.
He was keenly missed by all the family on the rare occasions that he was away from home.

CHAPTER FIVE

THE
HAPPIEST YEARS

More than husband and consort, Albert was everything to Victoria, and Osborne was unthinkable without him. It seemed to her that his quick active step was everywhere and she looked lovingly on his creation: 'I get fonder and fonder of it, one is so quiet here, and everything is of interest, it being so completely my beloved one's creation, – his delight and pride.'[1] Albert – 'happily engrossed in his occupations'[2] – planted trees, thinned them out, rejoiced at their growth, mourned their loss by frost or storm, trimmed, measured, planned, consulted, improved. He decided upon heathers for the pots in front of their door, bronze Venuses to play in the fountains on the terraces, and Britannic lions to guard the steps down to the lawns. When Albert was not superintending or directing, he 'helped'. He helped his wife when she copied a painting by Foltz; he helped the dachshunds dig for moles; he got down from the carriage when the drag broke and helped the gentlemen to free it; he took off his jacket and pulled a rowing boat down the beach so the Queen could be rowed about in the cool of the evening; he let off balloons for the children; he even turned the first somersaults in twenty years in the hay at the top of the valley footpath to show the nine-year-old Bertie how they were done.

He took Bertie with him to bathe and when he went to shoot partridge in the stubble fields; he let off balloons for the children and joined in their games; he arranged a parure of rubies and diamonds for Victoria; he drove her of an afternoon, or cantered along beside her carriage with a child or two, bursting with pride, riding beside him.

He consulted his artistic adviser, Ludwig Gruner, about decoration and the placing of some of the statues; he found time to give sittings to various painters for his portrait; he continued to select pictures for the newest parts of the house, and took pride in showing off his creation. Osborne was visited by

The Queen's birthday table in 1854, by James Roberts. For much of her married life the Queen's birthday was celebrated at Osborne. Every year Albert devised thoughtful surprises for his delighted wife, who would enter the present room with as much anticipation as a child.

some of the foremost establishment artists and arts' administrators of Albert's day, not only English, such as Sir Charles Eastlake, who was to become the first director of the National Gallery, but also foreigners like Professor Wagen, head of the Berlin Museum, and the 'celebrated' sculptor C.D. Rauch. For his birthday in 1851, the Queen gave Albert a statue of Victory by Rauch, a copy of the one in the Walhalla at Ratisbon. It was placed in the principal corridor, in a niche beside a window, where it can still be found today. The Queen would note approvingly that their visitors were delighted with all they saw.

When the Queen was grieved and distressed after hearing of the death of a

Queen Victoria holding a portrait of her beloved Albert, photograph by B.E. Duppa, July 1854. She relied on him utterly, and looked for his approval in everything from the set of her bonnets to the course of foreign policy.

relative it was Albert who took her out for a little soothing air. If he was not planning a new fountain, he was altering the layout of garden paths – Osborne, said the Queen, was the spot where Albert was happiest and the days when he was away seemed long and lonely. Increasingly he travelled great distances from the Isle of Wight to lay foundation stones of museums and hospitals, to inspect and to speak to the organizations of which he was patron. In this respect, he set a pattern of public service and royal patronage which is still in place today. And every night he returned to Queen Victoria.

On the morning of a birthday, it was Albert who checked that all was

Prince Albert, photograph by B. E. Duppa, May 1854. As husband of the sovereign, he occupied a uniquely difficult position; he was king of her heart, but was regarded with xenophobic prejudice by most of her subjects.

Prince Albert consciously set out to mould the Queen, and reform the aspects of her character which he felt needed improvement. Victoria always looked up to Albert but in some respects her reliance on him undermined her own self-confidence. Photographs by J. J. E. Mayall, 1860 (*left*) and Miss Day, 1859 (*right*).

ready in the present room before 'The Birthday' was fetched. From 1848 to 1861 the Queen was always at Osborne for her birthday on 24 May, a private, family celebration after the official one a few days before in London. Albert's birthday on 26 August fell less often at Osborne, being a time of year when they were often travelling abroad. It was a day which the Queen always greeted with a passionate thankfulness. 'Again I hail this blessed day', she wrote, 'which has given me the dearest, best, and purest of beings.'[3] She invariably awoke to the strains of his Christmas Hymn being played by the band under their window, and 'most tenderly and warmly' wished him joy while the band played on, from his favourite *Prophète* perhaps, or a 'pot pourri of German songs',[4] or 'a very fine chorale from Elijah'.[5] One year, as soon as Albert had gone to his dressing room, all the children came and sang before the door. Meanwhile, the Queen would put on a smart new gown, something fresh and summery, an embroidered muslin over pink, or a new lilac *mousseline de soie*, and see that everything was ready before hastening to fetch Albert from his room and take him to the present room. This was usually upstairs in the Main Wing, but occasionally his presents were laid out in the Horn Room in the Pavilion. In this grisly apartment, next door to the billiard room, all the furniture, from candlesticks and chandeliers to couch and chairs, was made of German stags' horns which Albert had bought in 1846.[6]

Outside the present room all the children would be waiting with nosegays for their father, the older girls in smart muslins, the boys in sailor suits, the younger children dressed up for the occasion. When Lenchen was four and Louise two and a half, they stood side by side in front of the presents 'dressed as cherubs in blue and pink crape, with little wings, and wreaths of roses and forget-me-nots in their hair. They looked very sweet,' wrote the Queen, 'holding up a card on which was inscribed "All blessing and happiness".'[7] Two years later, little Arthur, destined from the first for the army, appeared at the age of two in the 'complete uniform of an officer of the Scotch [sic] Fusiliers, in which he looked so funny and amused his father very much'.[8] Even Beatrice as a babe in arms, attending her father's birthday celebrations for the first time, was 'delightful in a pink and white cap',[9] a few years later 'running up to meet her Papa, a nosegay in her hand, and saying "many happy *turns* Papa".'[10] The children always worked hard in preparation for the day. They drew and painted pictures, worked slippers, or wrote out poetry on lace-edged paper in their best handwriting, 'everything they could think of to please their dear father'[11] – though the Queen noticed with regret how the elder boys as they grew up dropped this practice. Often the children would recite some French poetry, composed by their governess for the occasion.

The children expressed their devotion to Albert in 'great exertions', the Queen in a lavish giving of costly gifts, many of which were intended for Osborne, and stayed there. They were an eclectic mixture; in 1846, she bowed to her husband's highbrow taste for early Italian masters and gave him the glowing panels of Perugino's *St Jerome* and Bernardo Daddi's *Sposalizio* (then attributed to Agnolo Gaddi), and which Albert eventually hung in his dressing room. Among the silver and ornaments for the house, and more to her own taste, was the portrait of Baghdad, Albert's 'fine black horse' by J.F. Herring, which was hung in her dressing room, one of a large menagerie of animal paintings which she was to commission. If something had caught Albert's eye during the year, the Queen would try to buy it for him. In 1845 they had visited the Duke of Buckingham at Stowe, where Albert admired 'an antique Venus', one of the classical statues in the Pompeian Drawing Room, which the Duke himself had seen dug up from the baths of Caracalla in Rome.[12] The Duke kept such regal state that in 1848 he was obliged to auction off the contents of his house to pay his debts and the Queen considered herself lucky enough to be able to buy Albert his *Venus Anadyomene*, the goddess of love rising from the sea, sensuously running her hands through her long hair – what a gift for a Queen to give the man who was her 'all in all'. The Venus arrived a little too late to attend the Prince's birthday table, but took her place among the growing crowd of mythical figures in the principal corridor.

The Queen gave Albert modern statuary. In 1850 she gave him *The Huntress* by R.J. Wyatt, 'whose recent death', said Victoria, 'is so much to be deplored'.[13] The first version of the work had been done for the King of Naples. The nymph and her hound, from whose paw she extracts a thorn, went to live in the billiard room but the Queen took up to her sitting room, where she would see it every day, a painting she gave Albert at the same time which she thought was 'perhaps one of Winterhalter's most charming pictures'.[14] It showed Victoria sitting on the terrace at Osborne, with Arthur in his long baby clothes lying in her lap. Franz Xaver Winterhalter, from the Black Forest, was perhaps one of the last great court painters; under his magical brush every woman became a beauty, every man a hero, every child, as the Queen might have said, a charming rosebud. Victoria and Albert patronized him enthusiastically, keeping him busy with their ever-increasing family.

The painting that dominated the Queen's sitting room was a large composition by Winterhalter called *Florinda*, which the Queen gave Albert for his birthday in 1852. It shows a group of plump nudes amusing themselves in a

Prince Arthur in the uniform of the Scots Fusiliers, by Winterhalter, 1852. Arthur was born on the birthday of the Duke of Wellington, who was his godfather, and from the first the child was destined for the army.

Florinda, by Winterhalter, was one of the Queen's birthday presents to Albert in 1852. She called it 'splendid and delightful' (RA QVJ, 18 July 1854), and it hung in her sitting room. Winterhalter later used the same composition for his painting of the Empress Eugénie and her Ladies.

dappled glade, loosely based on a rare moment of peace in a blood-boltered narrative poem, *Roderick the Last of the Goths*, by Robert Southey. It was perhaps a surprisingly sensual gift, a frank enjoyment of the female body, for the Queen to give her husband, not one which most people would associate with her later, umbrous image. It could be that she, who responded very strongly to physical beauty, enjoyed the painting more than her husband, for Albert was notoriously immune to feminine charms. It has been suggested that this was a result of his first-hand experience of the catastrophic effects of sexual licence; first, as a child whose mother had been forced to leave him as a direct result of her adultery; and later, when he witnessed the effects of venereal disease which left his brother Ernest sterile.

The presents that Victoria and Albert gave one another at Osborne were not exclusively for or about Osborne; the royal couple had recently discovered Scotland, and a Highland flavour crept into the present-giving; in 1850 in the form of a painting by Landseer, another of the Queen's favourite painters, which she described, momentarily dipping her pen in Scottish ink, as 'a "Lassie" crossing a burn with fawns'. She glowed with Albert's praise for her choices: 'Albert was delighted with his presents and at possessing these various, so individual, "chef d'oeuvres" of these different distinguished artists.'[15] Later in the day she went to look at her own bust carved by Gibson, which she artlessly classified as 'really beautiful. I consider him a great artist and completely unprejudiced. He deplores the lack of taste in this country, but says that Albert has already done a great deal to improve art, and by degrees to raise the whole standard.'[16] Anyone who approved of Albert was of course completely unprejudiced.

Gibson's bust of the Queen was among her presents to Albert in 1851, when another Winterhalter charted the progress of young Arthur who had slipped from the Queen's lap since Albert's last birthday, and in this year's charming offering was crawling along after a ball, trailing his long clothes behind him.

Hardly a birthday went by without the Queen giving Albert some image of herself; accompanying *Florinda* was a double portrait, also by the prolific Winterhalter, of Victoria and her cousin Victoire, the Duchess of Nemours. Winterhalter was as much a magician as the elderly Andreoletti; the double portrait is imbued with a fugitive nostalgia, the painter's sleight of hand appearing to interrupt the cousins, side by side on a gilded seat, exchanging thoughtful confidences in a never-never landscape. Albert professed himself 'greatly pleased' with both Winterhalters, but he hung them in rooms he shared with the Queen: *Florinda* went up on the wall of the Queen's sitting room (initially without a frame[17]) and *The Cousins* in the Queen's bedroom, not his own sanctuary — in Albert's room, which was almost entirely devoted to the grave beauty of his religious Italian masters, there was no place for lush images of the Queen, nor for such touching portraits as the little Winterhalter sketch of Arthur in his guard's uniform which the Queen put on Albert's table in 1853.

Such portraits, visible at every turn to the Queen in her private apartments, put a romantic gloss on the turbulent reality of their subjects, and were intimate and private belonging to the closed world of the Queen and her family. The more formal of the paintings which Victoria heaped on Albert's Osborne present tables were scattered all over the house and finding suitable spots for them, 'always a difficult task',[18] provided occupation for winter mornings when it was too wet for Victoria and Albert to get out for their constitutional. The *Assunta d'Albano* by Riedel, which she gave him in 1853 together with a view of Constantinople by Jacob Jacobs, they decided would look very well in the drawing room, though the Jacobs later found its way upstairs to her sitting room. Another painting from the same birthday harvest, *Napoleon Crossing the Alps* by Hippolyte Delaroche, went down to the other end of the Main Wing to the sitting room in the visitors' suite known as the Duchess of Kent's rooms.

The themes remained constant; on his table in 1854 Albert found yet another Winterhalter, this time of Leopold, as a pendant to the one of Arthur and the ball, and a painting by the German Carl Haag of Affie being carried across the River Dee by one of the ghillies. In 1856 the Queen gave Albert a surpassing miscellany:

. . . a picture of myself, in uniform, on horseback, as a pendant to the one of Albert, a beautiful French cabinet, inlaid with plaques of china, a bust of the Maharajah [Dhuleep Singh, deposed heir of the Punjab, a protegé of Victoria and Albert's] by Marochetti (which I think entirely spoilt, by being coloured) – the remainder of the dessert service for Balmoral, and a mechanical piano.[19]

When the presents had been viewed, explained, and exclaimed over, the whole family went down to breakfast. Out in the bay the yachts would be lying at anchor, decked out with flags, and the band would play at every meal. After luncheon the Queen and Prince would usually listen to the children playing their pieces but in 1852 the children presented their father with a surprise tableau, a kind of domesticated descendant of the court masque which had once entertained their forebears. The Queen described how 'a little stage and green frame, had been admirably arranged at the end of the Council Room, which was entirely darkened. The curtain was drawn aside, showing the six children, grouped to represent Milton's *Allegro* and *Penseroso*, the latter personified by Vicky, as a nun, quite in black.'[20] They were grouped among orange trees, corn, and fruit. All had bare feet except Vicky, as Melancholy, at twelve getting a little old for such informality. Her brothers and sisters personified various pastoral aspects of Joy in characters which were distant cousins of the statues in the drawing room; Bertie, with his panpipe was again a shepherd-like figure, and Affie seemed unable to shake off the doubtful grape, today wreathed in his hair to signify Plenty. Lenchen and Louise in yellow and blue gauze, 'looking charming', and Alice 'extremely pretty', leaning on Vicky, in her fair hair a wreath of cornflowers, which would have matched the blue of her eyes. The Queen, who had been in on some of the long rehearsals, was much pleased:

It was a great surprise to Albert who was delighted; and could not imagine how it had been so well contrived. As is usual the curtain was drawn and raised three times, and Albert asked for a fourth time. There followed (which was quite a surprise to *me*) three other groupings in succession each repeated twice and each charming. The children stood so still. Our people had arranged everything so well, and everyone has taken such pains. Mr Becker played a little accompaniment each time.[21]

Programme for the concert which concluded Albert's birthday in 1852. 'All went off extremely well', wrote the Queen in her journal for the day, 'and almost all the pieces were new and pretty. Formes never sang better and Die Thräne was more beautiful than ever.'

Usually some of the children would appear at dinner, perhaps in the fancy dress they had worn to attend the present table. The Queen might wear some of the jewellery Albert had given her, and as it grew dark they would watch the yachts in the bay light up and a blaze of fireworks, rockets, and coloured lights shoot up from the shore and the grounds. Often there was a concert after dinner, with almost all the pieces 'new and pretty'; in 1851 they heard Mr Roberts, the Welsh harpist; in 1852, they had a concert of leading opera singers; in 1856 they heard Signor Piatti play the violincello ('quite beautiful'), and Signor Siglicelli the violin ('very good'), and Signor Bianchi ('pianoforte, also good'). In 1854 they rang the changes with 'a very entertaining evening', provided by Albert Smith, the humourist turned popular entertainer, who gave them the pleasure of a private performance of his wildly successful 'lecture' the *Ascent of Mont Blanc*, and anecdotes of the English travelling abroad. His royal audience thought his imitations were most amusing and were kept 'in fits of laughter'; but best of all the Queen liked his duet between the piano and cornet, and the piece on the bad French spoken in restaurants.[22] If the day ended in a beautiful still evening there was every chance of a country dance on the terrace. The sound of the band would have floated down to the sailors on the yachts riding at anchor in the bay and echoed among the groves of Albert's plantations. Her beloved one would thank the Queen 'so kindly and affectionately' for all that she had given him and arranged for him and the 'dear day' generally ended 'as it began, in that love and affection which makes our life together such a blessed one'.[23]

On the occasions when Albert was not at Osborne, but some of his very young children were, the guardians of the nursery would try to instil a festive air in the day. They made wreaths for the children, who, dressed in their best, put nosegays at the naked feet of the statue of Albert, where they found little presents for themselves – drums, dolls' furniture, a white dog, a windmill – and then went out on to the lawn to run around and listen to the band. Such excitement invariably ended in disaster, with overexcited princesses throwing tantrums.[24]

Albert's birthday was also celebrated with a rural fête which the Queen gave to all the labourers on the estate. The first was in 1846, when Cubitt's

The first rustic fête at Osborne, *Illustrated London News*, 1846. This celebration of Albert's birthday became an annual institution for the people who lived on the estate.

The fête was an occasion which Victoria always enjoyed; in 1849 she painted the scene.

workmen were included. There were at that time forty-four men and boys in regular employment in the gardens, woods, and on Barton Farm, with a further six men on piecework; Cubitt's workmen swelled the numbers to some 250, a total which remained steady, when in subsequent years, after Cubitt's contract came to an end, the sailors of the royal yacht took part. At three o'clock in the afternoon, the royal family went out to watch the proceedings on the flat piece of lawn between the new house and Osborne Cottage, where the revellers were already seated at long tables drawn up in the shade of two large tents. Bright flags of different nationalities waved overhead, and the red and gold royal standard flew from the flagstaff on the Prince's new tower. The Bishop of Oxford said grace, the band of the 17th Regiment struck up with airs and favourite selections, and Victoria and Albert's workforce 'substantially regaled themselves' on 'a bountiful spread' of beef, mutton, vegetables and bread from the royal kitchen.[25] Copious supplies of beer flowed to drink the healths of the royal family who then withdrew, while the men enjoyed a pipe or two of the tobacco provided by Her Majesty. Later on, the royal family returned to sit on camp stools and watch the people 'dancing, playing at cricket, jumping in sacks, running races and other sports. I never saw so much fun', said the Queen, 'and people more cheery and pleased. The music, the happy people, shouting, laughing, dancing, and playing (without ever being disorderly), was a charming sight ... some of our footmen and grooms and one or two of the steward's room boys distinguished themselves greatly in running and jumping.'[26] The Queen always enjoyed the annual fête, but many of her Household did not. Lady Lyttelton, for instance, dismissed the afternoon as 'noisy, merry, and intensely boring, as usual. In the middle of the interminable country-dance on the green, nothing but footmen and housemaids pounding away their ale, and the yachts' crew running in sacks and dancing horn pipes.'[27]

The Queen greeted her own birthday with mixed feelings. It was a time for looking back and to the future, for remembering people who were no longer

Queen Victoria's birthday table for 1849 in the Horn Room, by J. Nash; above it, the two principal paintings given to the Queen. 'This day', ran the entry in her journal, 'was again welcomed in by the tender love and affection of my dearest Albert, whose care of me and unselfishness, seem yearly to increase.'

with her, and for anticipating the time when the children would begin to marry and the family circle would be broken up. One of the 'faults', which Albert attempted to cure her of, and failed, was the Queen's inability to live in the present. When she was happy she fended off the future by anticipating it; and dealt with change when it came by dwelling on the past. The band under her window would wake her with a hymn – 'Now thank we all our God', or Psalm 100 – while Albert wished her joy so tenderly, so merrily, so lovingly, that she confessed humbly: 'Often I feel surprised at being *so* loved, and tremble at my great happiness, dreading that I may be *too* happy.'[28]

In a new summer dress, a green barège embroidered with red rosebuds, or muslin embroidered in pink, often a present from her mother, she was taken by Albert to the present room, either the Horn Room, the Council Room before it was finished, or, later, through the upper colonnade to a room upstairs in the Main Wing, where all her children, beside themselves with anticipation, awaited her with birthday wishes and bouquets of lilies of the valley and geraniums. Often the girls' dresses were trimmed with ribbons to match the colour the Queen was wearing. 'It is a touching and a happy sight for me', said Victoria, 'to see our dear children all together, all at their different ages, and such days as this are always full of emotions.'[29] Excitement was uppermost as the Queen rustled into her present room in her new gown: 'It is always a delightful moment going into the room where my presents are', she said, 'and I have still the same feeling I had as a child.'[30] She had good reason; there would be wreaths of violet field orchids round the table and the whole room would be decked out with swags and garlands of flowers and greenery, flags, and doves in gilded cages, and the initials of the family wreathed around decorated pillars or looped across the front of present tables laden with gifts. The children drew, painted, and wrote out verses for her, just as they did for their father, old aunts sent their needlework, and Albert showered her with paintings, sculptures, and objets d'art.

Victoria was especially pleased with the presents prepared for her thirtieth birthday, in 1849, 'just what I particularly like and so kindly thought out'.[31] No less than four Winterhalters were exchanged on that day. He had painted a portrait of the Duchess of Kent which she gave her daughter who thought it 'a charming and wonderful likeness'. From Albert came another, of Affie and Lenchen, 'wonderfully like', in Highland dress tussling over a handful of eagle feathers. The Queen herself had commissioned two as surprises for Albert: Bertie and Affie in Highland dress with a devoted terrier, and three-year-old Lenchen, swamped under the helmet of Minerva, the Goddess of Wisdom and War. As if Winterhalter's painted riches were not enough, there was a circular locket in rubies and diamonds, in which to place 'dear Albert's and all the children's hair', and a sleepy statue, *La Filatrice Addormentata*, by the German sculptor Troschel. The Duchess of Kent was put up above the door in the dining room for a trial period – the Queen thought it rather too dark a spot – and stayed there until she was taken down in 1902, and replaced with a copy which hangs there today. Lenchen and Affie were hung in the drawing room and the Lenchen Minerva was put in Victoria's sitting room. Lenchen was very proud of her helmet. Later that year, Louise got hold of it, stalking about in it and looking 'too funny' so that the Queen could not resist putting a little sketch of the child in her diary.

The Queen was so delighted with Winterhalter's portraits of the Duchess of Kent (see p. 16) and Lenchen with Affie that she herself painted miniature copies for her journal.

OPPOSITE: Lenchen and Affie, by Winterhalter, which Albert gave to the Queen for her birthday in 1849.

129

Lenchen in the helmet of Minerva, by Winterhalter, one of the two 'surprises' which the Queen had arranged for Albert on her own thirtieth birthday.

'Louise is as proud of the helmet as Lenchen and stalks about in it, looking too funny', wrote the Queen when she added this sketch to her journal for 11 December 1849.

OPPOSITE: Louise, Arthur and Leopold, by Winterhalter, given to the Queen by Albert in 1856.

Every year the gifts came splendid and numerous, and only occasionally did Victoria unconvincingly protest that they were far too much, and she really could not have them all. As always, though, the presents to which the Queen gave most attention, were the paintings and statues of her family. Albert did not return her habitual birthday compliment to him with portraits of himself but he did indulge her with versions of their children in marble and paint, like the statue which he gave her in 1853, by the Italian Carlo Marochetti, of the three-year-old Arthur holding a sword supposedly belonging to his illustrious godfather, which thereafter stood guard in the corridor outside the Council Room. He heaped upon her Bacchic heads; busts of classical worthies – and unworthies – from Euripides to Caligula; and paintings and statues inspired by such diverse poets as Goethe and Robert Burns. All these were 'charming', but the Queen declared that nothing could have given her more pleasure than the portfolio of crimson velvet which Albert gave her in 1854 containing coloured photographs of the five tableaux of the Seasons, which the children had enacted earlier in the year in honour of their parents' wedding anniversary. 'I was really delighted', said the Queen, 'and could not express *all* I *felt*.'[32] Albert achieved another coup in 1856 aided by Winterhalter, who had painted Louise, Arthur and Leopold; 'such a lovely picture, with so much light and freshness about it.'[33] Best of all, it was a surprise. This was hung in the dining room. Another of Albert's principal presents that year 'was a lovely tiara, necklace, brooch and earrings in light gold filigree work with pearls in the centre, from the Paris exhibition.'[34] The Queen was just as pleased with the fan which Vicky had painted for her, with emblems of the initials of all the family.[35]

She would sometimes venture a gift in return, as a souvenir of the day, like the miniature by Ross of three of their children which she gave Albert with some trepidation in 1853, reporting with relief that he 'could hardly believe Ross could have done such a painting. I owned to the original idea being mine, and had been nervously anxious that he should approve, knowing what a judge he is and what taste he has!'[36] The consciously didactic lead which Albert gave the Queen in so many areas actually undermined her self-confidence.

Historical paintings, marble nymphs for the sculpture gallery, life-size bronze Seasons for the terrace, a French fan, a dress each year from Mama; the themes were constant, but it was always the pictures of the children which the Queen singled out: the 'lifesize heads of Lenchen and Louise, encircled by a wreath of lilies, very prettily painted in oils, by Sant, and a beautiful coloured photograph of the dear little baby in her cradle' which Albert gave her in 1857.[37] Her elder daughters became more proficient, and more ambitious; in the same year Vicky gave her a watercolour of a scene from *Richard II*, Bolingbroke's entry into London, which she had taken nearly two months to do, getting up early in the morning to paint it. The Queen thought it 'quite worthy of a first rate artist', and had it hung in her bedroom.[38] All over Osborne went the tokens of the love and esteem of the Queen's family; wherever the Queen went the substantial mementoes were there to remind her of her great happiness.

The Queen's thirtieth was a typically tranquil birthday. During breakfast:

. . . the Band played and the children played about very happily. After breakfast the Ladies and Gentlemen came over and all, admired my presents. We then walked out with the four eldest children, and took them to see the sheep shearing, going

afterwards along a new footpath in the wood where they busily picked quantities of flowers. The day brilliantly fine, and very hot in the sun. We remained out some little time longer, under the trees. All seemed so smiling, so bright and beautiful.[39]

It was just the day to superintend the hanging up, '*at last*', of the vast canvas known as the 'family picture', which Winterhalter had completed some two years earlier. He had preserved a glowing period in the Queen's life which became for the Queen an icon of her life with her husband; now, every meal in the dining room was taken below a serene young couple wreathed in what Lady Lyttelton called '*perfect, awful*, spotless prosperity' with their pretty children

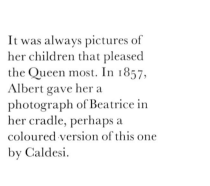

It was always pictures of her children that pleased the Queen most. In 1857, Albert gave her a photograph of Beatrice in her cradle, perhaps a coloured version of this one by Caldesi.

playing harmoniously at their feet. When the painter visited Osborne, the Queen did him the rare honour of taking him herself to see how his pictures looked, and a copy of the 'family picture' hangs in the same place today.

On her birthday, between the tree planting, the answering of an avalanche of letters of congratulation, the visits to the sheep shearing at Barton, and being photographed on the terrace ('the instantaneous process' which could miraculously seize and fix motion[40]) there was still time for surprises, like the year that the Duchess of Kent arranged for a group of Tyrolean singers to perform at breakfast. When Vicky was nine and Alice was seven they were dressed up in the costume of the 1740s, and danced a minuet before their mother, 'Vicky made a capital boy and looked so tall and dignified, Alice so refined and graceful and her figure looked lovely. The powder was very becoming to both. It was dearest Albert's surprise for me, and I was *so* pleased and touched.'[41] It was the same when the Queen listened to the children playing the pieces they had learnt for the day, like the quintet on airs composed by Albert, which had been arranged by Cusins, in which Vicky and Lenchen played one piano, Bertie and Alice another, and Affie, the violin:[42] Queen Victoria saw their hard work to give her pleasure as an expression of their affection.

Wherever Albert was, there was also music; and at Osborne he and the Queen could savour more than just the 'stolen moments' which were all they could catch in London or at Windsor. Here the Queen could practise her piano or her singing for an hour at a time, sometimes before breakfast, sometimes

Winterhalter's sketch for the 'Family Picture', 1847, which became a central icon at Osborne. It is carefully and symbolically posed: Bertie, the Queen's heir stands at her knee, holding a sceptre (removed in the final version), looking up at his father who may just be on the point of issuing a 'dear reprimand' or checking Affie's uncertain steps. To the left are grouped his daughters, Alice, Lenchen, and Vicky.

duets with Albert after luncheon, perhaps trying out 'a new and beautiful symphony by Mendelssohn, which has only just been arranged for two performers. It is called "La Salterella" and we heard it at the Philharmonic. I must say', added the Queen rather ambiguously, 'it was wonderful how it went.'[43]

The music at Osborne was by no means all of their own making. Frequently there were concerts after dinner, quite private, and not necessarily when there were any special guests. They generally took place in the Council Room, beginning at a little before ten o'clock. Singers of international reputation, fresh from successes in the latest operatic triumphs from Paris to St Petersburg, performed for the private delectation of the Queen and her consort. Besides the Queen's old favourite, Lablache, there was the tenor Giovanni Matteo Mario, who had once been an officer in the Sardinian Army, before his

revolutionary politics forced him into exile and he took up a singing career. The Queen had seen him sing John of Leiden in Meyerbeer's hugely successful opera, *Le Prophète*, which had brought its composer wealth and acclaim throughout Europe. Mario had a rich, powerful voice; 'the feeling, fire, and facility of his singing,' said the Queen (and we can hear a ghostly echo of Albert in her words), 'really touches one to hear.'[44] When Mario sang at Osborne he still looked much as he did in the opera, bearded, and with his hair parted down the centre; his head, thought the Queen, was 'quite une tête de Christ'.[45] Another political exile was the German bass, Karl Johann Formes, whose 'fine countenance' and 'nice frank manner' met with royal approval, as did the sweet-voiced, 'pleasing and ladylike' French soprano, Jeanne Anais Castellan. At these concerts the singers were accompanied on the piano by the conductor and composer Michael Costa, a leading light in the world of London's music.

Victoria and Albert fully appreciated the quality of these performers and did not waste any opportunity to hear them. They attended rehearsals in the afternoon, afterwards talking to the singers about the pieces they had heard and about the newest operas by composers such as Wagner. On one occasion, Mario and Formes tried out a piece that Meyerbeer had sent the Queen entitled 'Ode to Rank'. It was not a success; in the Queen's delicate phrase, it 'did not strike us as being very fine'.[46] The evening's programme usually consisted of favourite arias and duets from opera – in the early 1850s, this meant mostly Meyerbeer: the duet from his *Huguenots*, for instance, or the pastorale from *Le Prophète* – punctuated with works by Paer, Schubert, and Bellini. Such concerts, said the Queen, were 'a great treat'.[47]

OPPOSITE: Opportunities for dressing up were frequent, and a source of much pleasure. On the Queen's birthday in 1850 Albert arranged a surprise: Alice and Vicky danced before her in eighteenth-century costumes; watercolour by Winterhalter.

BELOW LEFT: Arthur (left) and Alfred in the costume of Sikh princes, photograph by Dr E. Becker, 1854.

BELOW RIGHT: It was Affie's own idea to learn the violin, and he would play it in the little concerts which the children performed on their parents' birthdays; photograph by Roger Fenton, 8 February 1854.

The last of the Queen's birthday tables at Osborne in 1861, by Roberts. Of this year's presents, she singled out for mention in her journal a portrait of her mother, a Belgian landscape, and the 'pretty things' her children had embroidered, painted, or drawn for her.

During much of 1850 and 1851, Albert was preoccupied with his latest project, the Great Exhibition. He became absorbed in conversation with learned professionals and was late for dinner with the Queen. Items of interest in the house, such as the eight-foot high glass candelabras made by Osler of Birmingham to a design which the Prince had had a hand in deciding, and which normally stood on either side of the drawing-room fireplace (where they still are today), were packed up and sent to the Crystal Palace for exhibition. Among the visitors drawn to London by the great event were the Prince and Princess of Prussia and their son Frederick, known in the family as Fritz, who Victoria and Albert already had their eye on as a future husband for Vicky. She was still only eleven, and of course quite unaware of their plans for her. The Prussians were invited to Osborne for the Queen's birthday, and contributed to her birthday table the contorted bronze statue of a boy and a swan, a copy of an antique statue in the Berlin Museum, which can still be seen on the Upper

Prince Albert, by
Winterhalter, 1855. Albert
had to earn his place in the
cultural life of England.
The success of the Great
Exhibition gave him new
standing.

Terrace. Even when the Exhibition was over, the gentlemen of the Executive
Committee came down to Osborne and were closeted away with Albert settling
the plans for what was to become the Victoria and Albert Museum, built from
the proceeds.

The Queen was certain that the Great Exhibition – a thrilling monument
to progress – would immortalize Albert's dearest name. To mark the great
event he gave her a watercolour by David Roberts of the transept of Paxton's
great glass cathedral, which went up to her sitting room. The Privy Purse
recorded a huge bulge in the amount paid out on furniture at this time, for items
like the circular table in the drawing room, improvingly ornamented with
representations of temperance, the elements, and science.

As always, Victoria enthusiastically supported her husband, and on their
next visit to Osborne after the Exhibition was dismantled, they found
themselves confronted by 'quantities of things and presents'[48] – yet more hefty

mementoes of the Queen's adoration of everything that was Albert. The large sculptural group depicting Theseus and the Amazons by the Hungarian-born Joseph Engel, one of the colony of sculptors working in Rome, would look very well at the bottom of the staircase in the Pavilion, but where, for example, was a suitable spot for a pair of Sèvres vases depicting the triumph of Agriculture? For the bronze figurine of Joy, or for a garden seat designed by Ludwig Gruner and entirely carved out of coal?

While they were trying to find places for all their new acquisitions the Queen heard that there were 215 German emigrants stranded in East Cowes. They were bound for America, but their ship had been damaged, and they would have to wait several weeks while it was being repaired. The Queen immediately did her duty by them; John Blandford, her Clerk of the Works, doled out coffee, soup, and soap; the royal children made a collection of their old toys for the emigrant children; Marianne Skerrett, one of the Queen's dressers, was sent to take them wool, warm petticoats, and some stockings; and Albert's Private Secretary superintended the distribution of other clothing which the Queen bought for them. Victoria showed her usual curiosity about other people, going to New Barn in person to see the beneficiaries of her charity, and much disappointed to find they were not there, having gone to church. She came again the next day and regarded them with just as much interest as they must have done her. The emigrants became a talking point at dinner, where it was explained to the Queen that the superior merits of the English Emigration Act would never have allowed such a situation to occur. The royal party left Osborne in a philanthropic glow; two cheering lines of Germans saw them down the hill and waved them off from Trinity Pier: 'Poor things', said the Queen, 'it must have given them a pang to see their protectors go.'[49]

Even at Osborne, Victoria and Albert were kept up to the minute with news of home and foreign affairs. While the emigrants had been drinking their coffee in the frosty open air, Victoria in the Pavilion had received the news, tapped through to England from France on the new submarine telegraph, that Louis Napoleon Bonaparte had staged a coup d'état in Paris. The immediacy of the news heightened its dramatic impact; 'the whole is like a Romantic play!' exclaimed the Queen,[50] not at all amused, and wondering how it would end. She would have been even more disagreeably startled if she had been told that within five years the parvenu emperor Napoleon III would be her welcome guest at Osborne. For the royal Household, however, only echoes of the outside world reached the shores of Albert's woods. The red boxes came and went, and their contents were discussed by Victoria and Albert in private; the Household were left to read the reflection of great events in the royal faces, or wait until the *Elfin* brought the newspapers. Occasionally, a tangible earnest of world events and technological progress arrived at the house: the largest piece of gold yet discovered in the Australian goldfields; a working model of a submarine (which unfortunately sank while its

The Queen, deeply interested, made these sketches of the Chinese family who, having visited the Great Exhibition, were presented to her at Osborne. She thought the bound feet of the ladies painful to see, but was impressed with the family's dignified good manners.

inventor was showing it to Albert); or a smooth-tongued diplomat who sat next to the Queen at dinner and enthralled her with faintly scandalous anecdotes of the moribund Ottoman Empire; or again, men of action who brought her eyewitness accounts of peoples they had encountered – Eskimos, Zulus, Bushmen, and Hottentots – at the frontiers of an expanding world.

The windows and terraces of Osborne, high up above the sea, provided Victoria and Albert with a splendid grandstand from which to view some spectacular natural phenomena which happened their way. The Queen first saw the aurora borealis at Osborne; she gasped at hailstones as big as walnuts which thumped onto the lawns in the summer of 1852 and which Albert broke open to disclose the shreds of crystal inside; she watched falling stars after dinner with Albert and Vicky; joined in the excitement on the terrace one afternoon to peer through smoked glasses at an eclipse of the sun, shivering in the uncanny twilight; gloried in the view from her sitting room of bright, silvery

Naval Review at Spithead, 11 August 1853, by J. S. Robins. Her Britannic Majesty, on board the *Victoria and Albert*, inspects the fleet and watches a mock gunboat action.

The fleet sailing from Spithead for the Baltic, 11 March 1854, by Duncan. The Queen, on the *Fairy*, watched the 'wonderful, inspiriting and solemn sight', until the ships disappeared over the horizon. (RA QVJ, 11 March 1854)

moonrises over the sea; and for several nights followed the tracks of a splendid comet careering away through the heavens.

From 1853, as England drifted towards war with Russia in the Crimea, the Queen discovered that in her marine residence she also had front row seats, if not in the theatre of war itself, at least in the dressing room. On 11 August that year she and Albert steamed across to Spithead in the *Victoria and Albert* for the naval review. The Queen's pen overflowed with patriotic fervour as she recalled the animated scene for her journal, sweeping into it helter-skelter the thousands of spectators lining the shore, the 'steamers crowded to suffocation, plying in every direction, – sailing boats of every description and yachts out, this besides the noble fleet, which saluted on our approach.'[51] Sail had not quite given way to steam. The 'noble fleet', with which Victoria and Albert now put out to sea, was in reality a motley assembly which represented every craft in her navy's transition from sail to steam. The fleet staged a sea battle, stirring up fierce emotions in the bosom of their sovereign as she watched a scene of:

… intense interest and indescribable beauty. Six broadsides were given by the 'enemy' and answered by the fleet, being kept up for fully six or seven minutes. It was truly magnificent, – the smoke curling up, at times disclosing the high masts and rigging of the noble vessels, at other moments all being enveloped in clouds. The sailing vessels lowered some of their rigging to give the effect of having been hit.'[52]

Later, in the evening, sitting under an awning rigged up between the paddle boxes on the royal yacht, Victoria and Albert watched thirty-eight gunboats attack two steamers under incessant fire from their heavy guns and discharges of musketry. 'It was a beautiful sight and gave one quite an idea, of what a *real* attack of that kind must be', wrote the Queen at the end of 'a long, but most enjoyable day'.[53]

A week later the Queen had a taste of what it was like aboard a capital ship when she spent a day on the *Duke of Wellington*. Much of the magic evaporated; cinders and 'blacks' came down in showers from the funnels and the pitching from the swell made the Queen's head ache, and made her 'very uncomfortable'.[54] She was kept going by the interest and excitement of watching 900 men, at a word, run and climb to get up sail, and running backwards and forwards with the great guns, pulling three or four tons as though it were a toy; and by the 'striking effect'[55] of the men in the rigging with cutlasses drawn to repel boarders.

As war clouds gathered and threatened, it was thought expedient to send a British fleet to the Baltic to keep an eye on Russia. Victoria and Albert were at Osborne when it sailed in March 1854 and enjoyed another day of interesting, solemn, and 'inspiriting' moments. They went over to Spithead, where the ships that were about to sail were surrounded by every kind of craft: sailing boats, rowing boats, densely crowded steamers, and boats bringing stores and ammunition. All the officers who were going took their leave of the Queen, who accompanied her fleet, under sail before a fair wind ('which greatly enhanced the beauty of the scene'[56]), out towards St Helen's where the *Fairy* lay to and Victoria and Albert were able to watch the fifteen ships slowly pass close by with cheering crews and a fitful sun gilding their sails. Thrilling to the cheers of the men 'which went through one';[57] the Queen would not have missed such a sight for anything. 'Besides', she roundly declared, 'it was our duty to be there to give satisfaction, and I am sure every sailor's face seemed brightening as he cheered.'[58] As the great ships towered majestically past, the Queen's sharp eye for detail was glad to see that the figurehead on the *Duke of Wellington* was a good likeness of the ship's namesake – surely a 'harbinger of glory'. The man on the very top mast raised both his arms as the ship passed by. As she 'gazed and gazed, till the noble ships could scarcely be discerned on the horizon',[59] Victoria could not know that they were sailing off into a peripheral role in the war which followed.

Victoria had a strong personal feeling for the men in 'her' army and navy, and while at Osborne in January 1855 was surprised to see that a note she had written sending a message to Florence Nightingale had appeared in the papers. 'Startled as I was at first, it has called forth such very kind observations in the different papers, that I feel it may be the means of my *real* sentiments getting known by the army. Therefore I can no longer regret it.' Miss Nightingale had

Battlefield, Crimea,
watercolour by the Prince
of Wales, *c*.1855.

written that: 'The men were touched to the heart by the Queen's message,
saying that it was a very feeling letter, and with tears, that she was thinking of
them, – that each man ought to have a copy, which they would keep to their
dying day.'[60] Many men did not have long to wait for the final eventuality,
dying by their thousands in allied camps before Sebastopol.

A side-effect of hostilities had been the plight of two small Bulgarian boys,
exactly the same age as the Queen's two youngest boys Arthur and Leopold,
who had been left wounded and dying beside their dead parents on the beach at
Custëndje, victims of 'a party of Bashi Bazouks, prowling for plunder'.[61] They
were rescued and adopted by Captain Hyde Parker of HMS *Firebrand* who
brought them aboard his ship, where he and his sailors christened the children
John and George Firebrand, provided medical treatment for their wounds, a
goat to supply the infant with milk, and fought two engagements with the
Russian guns of Sebastopol. The gallant Captain added his own measure of
tragedy to the violent tale by falling 'shot through the heart' at the Sulina. It
was a story of mutilated innocence and soft-hearted men of derring-do such as
the Queen found irresistible, and she no sooner heard it than she announced her
wish to take the orphans under her wing. She consulted Toward as to who on
the estate would be most suitable to take charge of them, and at his suggestion
the boys went to Mrs Jackman, wife of one of the carters on the farm at Barton,
who kept the most spotlessly clean cottage on the estate.

The Queen went straight over to see them. In spite of the terrible scars left
by the five bullets through his right arm and the bad powder burns, Johnny was
'very merry and intelligent and speaks English perfectly'.[62] Little Georgy,
delicate and gentle, bore the scar of the bullet which had passed through his
infant wrist and killed his mother. The next time she came she brought her
sketchbook; the boys were at that stage when she most liked children, and their

youth gave them licence. When one of them stole her parasol when she was not looking and galloped off across the gravel using it as a hobby horse, she simply laughed, showing both her humility and humour. The boys were renamed John and George Hyde, and remained with the Jackmans until they joined the Navy.

Families on the Osborne estate who had sons serving in the Navy were luckier than most in one respect during the Crimean War; their employer was at least in a position to find out news of their sons, about whom they had heard nothing for months, and she promised to do so. Any news from the war was brought to the Queen at once. She was frequently brought despatches while she was still in bed, and was constantly in touch with the war. With Portsmouth so close, it was easy to go across and inspect a troopship taking cavalry to the Black Sea; the Queen patted the horses and observed that the men were wearing white smocks for the voyage. Dinner guests at Osborne began to include men who had been in the Crimea and could give harrowing accounts of 'the misery, the suffering, the total lack of everything, the sickness, etc.'[63] Some of these officers, often themselves lame and bent with rheumatism and exhausted from cholera and dysentery, spared Her Majesty few grisly details; how the men were up to their waists in frozen water in the trenches, how weak they were, how portions of feet came away with their boots. Others painted a suspiciously glowing account of improved conditions, of the marvellous new camps and hospitals, of noble, brave, unselfish, happy troops. Victoria's thankful, unquestioning cup brimmed over: 'Is this not a sufficient reward for *all* the constant anxiety I go through, and may I not indeed be *very proud* of these splendid fellows?'[64]

The table in Albert's room was spread with maps of the war zone, which the Prince and Queen pored over with visiting generals; they looked at Roger Fenton's photographs of camp and battlefield (which were criticized for presenting a sanitized view of the war); handsome, wounded officers were presented to the Queen and she was shown the 'comfortable' new knapsack which was to be issued to the troops. But all this was as nothing compared to the evening when they were out in the *Fairy* and came across a large steamer which turned out to be bringing home 420 sick and wounded. 'We hailed her', wrote the Queen, 'and went up close to her. In an instant her deck was crowded with invalid soldiers, in every kind of attire, with a most Crimean look, and long beards, who cheered us most heartily, evidently much pleased that their Queen should be the first to welcome them home. It quite moved me for it seemed to bring one quite into communication with that brave Army.'[65] Suddenly Osborne, 'besides its quiet and natural beauties', was '*full* of the *greatest* possible interest.'[66]

Interest and pride in her soldiers was adulterated with indignation at the conduct of her government. In 'lengthy and serious' audience she took Palmerston to task: 'The heedlessness of the Government in not seeing that everything is done *without fail*, to save all those precious lives, is too incomprehensible!'[67] She had had her personal worries, too, having been 'alarmed and perturbed'[68] when an outbreak of scarlatina was diagnosed in the nursery: 'The quarantine it will entail, the suspense and doubt we shall be in, are most trying, and I felt in a sort of state of despair.'[69]

No sooner was Victoria thanking God for bringing 'the dear children safely through this often most serious illness', the nursery having been

The elder of the two Bulgarian orphans, later renamed John Hyde, whom the Queen had taken under her wing and sent to Barton: 'Johnny is a dear, funny boy, and very good.' (RA QVJ, 18 March 1855) Sketch by the Queen, 19 March 1855.

thoroughly disinfected and all woollen things burnt, than a fresh set of problems cropped up. In the interests of allied solidarity, Victoria and Albert were to pay a state visit to the Emperor Napoleon III and his Spanish wife, Eugénie, during the Paris Exhibition. For days beforehand, all was preoccupation and bustle. The Queen became 'much troubled with questions of toilette and other arrangements';[70] and perhaps it was out under the trees of Osborne that she dreamt up the astonishing ensemble in which she entered Paris, shaded by a bright green parasol, wearing a plain straw bonnet, and a dress as full of geraniums as the flowerbeds on the Osborne terraces, while her reticule was emblazoned with a large white poodle. Vicky and Bertie were allowed to accompany their parents and for a few dazzling, giddy days the English royal

Guard's Hill, Church Parade, with Balaklava in the distance; photograph by Roger Fenton, 1855. Victoria and Albert kept in close touch with the progress of the war. They looked at Fenton's photographs of the Crimea at Osborne in August of that year.

family found themselves the centre of Paris *en fête*, before returning to Osborne, feeling 'very excited and unable to do anything but talk all day of everything we had seen and done.'[71] Thank-you letters flew to 'the dear Emperor and Empress', the presents brought back for the younger children were all distributed, and there was nothing left but to arrange their memories and read the flattering accounts from Paris: 'I was thought so dignified,' said the Queen, '"gracieuse", and was so well dressed (which considering all the trouble I took I am glad to hear).'[72] Alone together after dinner, they occupied themselves with sorting through prints and views of Paris, cut out the 'very good' engravings of the visit which the *Illustrated London News* had already published, and arranged them for pasting into the latest albums.

The war dragged on to its inconclusive peace treaty. In May 1856 the Queen went backwards and forwards from Osborne to Portsmouth, inspecting militia, laying the foundation stone of the Royal Victoria Military Hospital at

Netley, and visiting the 8th Hussars, just back from the Crimea, some of whom had taken part in the Charge of the Light Brigade. They were 'such fine, bronzed and bearded fellows', said the Queen admiringly,[73] and watched them go past with a swelling heart; 'at such moments I feel so very keenly the wish to be a man, and to be able to command *such* men!'[74] Characteristically oblivious to consistency, however, the Queen cast a wary eye on the 'celebrated' Mrs Duberley, who had published a journal of her wartime experiences with her husband, and decided she was 'rather masculine and fast, but perfectly well-behaved'.[75]

The routine crossing to Osborne was invested with great interest when the new *Victoria and Albert*, 100 feet longer than the old, and so big and magnificent that the Queen at first felt 'quite lost' in her, came upon ships crowded with troops, just arrived from the Crimea; 'the men cheered heartily', wrote the Queen, 'and touchingly clustering together to see us and I waved my

In the interests of allied solidarity, the Queen left Osborne for a state visit to Paris; her triumphal entry on 18 August 1855 is recorded here by E. Guerard. The visit cemented an already cordial personal relationship with the Emperor Napoleon III and his fascinating wife, the Empress Eugénie.

handkerchief as we passed close under the bows of the ship. Last year we only met sick and wounded – what a difference!'[76].

Odd flotsam and jetsam from the war turned up at Osborne. Some were predictable souvenirs, such as the two guns which were presented to the Queen on the beach; others less so, like the baby which had been born in the Crimea on the day of the Battle of Inkerman, and which was brought to Osborne to be shown to the Queen. She looked it over knowledgeably; it was paralysed down one side from exposure; and had been given a medal with two clasps, which the company had bought. The Queen gave the baby toys and some money. Also brought to Osborne was the 'Crimean cow', which had supplied the Headquarters with milk. 'A curious creature', said the Queen vaguely, 'half Hungarian, half Roman looking.'[77]

Victoria and Albert's nine children (the Queen was so proud of the number) were all together under their parents' roof for only the short period between Beatrice's birth and Vicky's wedding. From left to right: Alice, Arthur, Albert, Bertie, Leopold, Louise, Beatrice, the Queen, Affie, Vicky, Lenchen. Photograph by Caldesi, May 1857.

The Grand Duke Constantine, the uncle of the Tsar, provided a prickly postscript to the war by inviting himself to stay at Osborne in May 1857. He was accorded all due ceremony – a guard of honour drawn up on the lawn, the Council Room given over to him to use as his drawing room – but the Queen was definitely on her mettle. Her old royal yacht was obliged to fly the Russian flag when bringing him into Osborne Bay; the English felt that the Russians had stolen a march on them by arriving in full uniform, as though for a state, rather than a private, visit, and a remark over dinner which displayed an imperial disregard for the property of poor people, the Queen thought 'in very bad taste on the Grand Duke's part, who one could not exactly call well-bred'.[78] His attendants were indiscreet, and he himself attempted some ill-advised bargaining with the Queen's ministers. Victoria and Albert took him out for a cruise the next day. The Queen winced at the Russian flag flying from the foremast; the Grand Duke had enough tact to admire the new *Victoria and*

Albert ('as well he may', Her Majesty darkly noted), and the Queen salved her nettled patriotism with memories of the stirring sights she had witnessed in these waters over the last three years.

Barely had the echocs of the guns which saluted the departing Grand Duke died away, than the Queen received a letter which contained a far more welcome proposal; the Emperor Napoleon and the Empress Eugénie also wished to visit Victoria and Albert at Osborne, 'which will be very nice', said the Queen, 'and is sure to do great good'.[79] She was right. Except for the weather, in which the Queen was as powerless as any anxious hostess, the French visit was indeed an unqualified success, from the moment that Napoleon and Eugénie landed on the beach below the house on the morning of Affie's birthday. Albert had escorted them ashore from their ship, the Queen's

barge flying the Emperor's standard – a tricolor spotted with golden Napoleonic bees – and the Queen was waiting on the beach to welcome them with a 'warm embrace'. Eugénie's uncrring dress sense had struck just the right note for an informal visit; she was in a green silk travelling dress with a waterproof paletot, and a plain straw bonnet. The Emperor, too, was informal and appropriate in morning clothes. In an open carriage they all drove up to the house where a band and a guard of honour of Coldstreams was drawn up on the lawn. Victoria and Albert took their guests to their rooms, the Duchess of Kent's suite under the clock tower overlooking the terrace and the sea. Among the pictures in the apartment hung Delaroche's painting of Napoleon I crossing the Alps, which the great man's nephew would have recognized as a flattering compliment. Victoria and Albert waited for them in the Council Room (it was rare for the Queen to wait for anyone) and then took them to the dining room for breakfast. Afterwards they walked, and sat outside for the rest of the

Arrival of Napoleon III and the Empress Eugénie at Osborne, 6 August 1857, by Lodden. It was a most successful visit; personal friendship oiled the wheels of diplomacy, but the Queen did wish the weather could have been better.

morning, Albert, Napoleon, and the Prime Minister Lord Palmerston speaking openly of 'Principalities, difficulties, rapprochements, alliance, etc.'[80] in an atmosphere of great goodwill. After luncheon they separated, the Queen and Albert retiring to their rooms.

An evening drive together to Carisbrooke Castle, and it was time to dress for dinner. Eugénie set the fashion the world over, from the salons of Paris to the saloons of the Wild West; she appeared at dinner elegantly pastoral in a light

The Empress Eugénie, by Winterhalter, 1857. She charmed and dazzled Victoria and the two women became lifelong friends.

OPPOSITE: *The Emperor Napoleon III*, by Winterhalter, c.1859.

organdie dress, embroidered all over with violets, with a wreath to match in her auburn hair, and pearls. She was beautiful, chic, graceful and fun. Queen Victoria was enchanted and even the unsusceptible Albert was captivated; he became 'excessively fond of her', wrote the Queen without a trace of jealousy, 'and I think few, if any Princess, has pleased him as much'.[81] The Emperor, too, she had already remarked, had 'a wonderful power of attaching people to him'.[82] The truth was that the Empress was not a Princess, she was a high-born Spaniard who had used a combination of her beauty, wits, and good luck to win her husband, who himself was not born to the purple; but Victoria and Albert undoubtedly found this pair of arrivistes a refreshing change from the usual run of blue-blooded royalty: 'I know no royalties, who were less "gênant"',

approved the Queen,[83] deploying the expression she reserved for tiresome, boring people and occasions.

Over the next few days, so far as a spell of wet stormy weather would allow, Napoleon and Eugénie were shown all that Osborne had to offer. They walked down to the sea; they ventured out between downpours to plant trees by the Mount; they took the charabancs to Ryde; they were shown over the farm, the Swiss Cottage and the *Victoria and Albert* and they were taken up to the private apartments in the Pavilion. (It is a matter of speculation as to what Eugénie thought when she saw the *Florinda* on the wall of the Queen's sitting room, Winterhalter having recently used the same composition for a large painting of herself surrounded by her ladies-in-waiting.) A marquee was pitched on the lawn with a covered way leading out to it from the drawing room, and on the Saturday evening Victoria, Albert, Napoleon, Eugénie, their assembled suites and all the children, except Leopold and Beatrice, danced waltzes and quadrilles, ending with Sir Roger de Coverley, which Eugénie had particularly wished to dance; 'a very pretty dance and successful evening', thought the Queen.[84] The next morning Victoria and Albert went as usual to church at Whippingham while the Emperor attended Mass at Newport.

Napoleon and Eugénie were excellent guests, taking a detailed interest in everything they saw and paying particular attention to the royal children. On their chilly return from the *Victoria and Albert* in the open barge Eugénie took Arthur on her knee and wrapped him in her cloak and the boy later appeared dressed as a drummer and drummed for the imperial visitors. They watched the four eldest children dancing impromptu reels in the pleasure grounds to the music of bagpipes, and the Emperor played with the children at breakfast and showed them tricks; 'They have been so very kind to them and taken such notice of them, and the children are so fond of them. They quite adore the Empress and would do anything for her.'[85]

In the four days that Napoleon and Eugénie were at Osborne the atmosphere of political suspicion between England and France which had thickened and curdled in the aftermath of the Crimean War largely evaporated. Knotty problems of European diplomacy were unravelled, and Napoleon and the Queen's ministers emerged into the corridors of Osborne wreathed in smiles; how providential it was that he had come, what a great advantage was personal communication! How very good it was to unite

Arthur and Leopold, by the Queen, about 1857. The French visitors won the children's hearts as well as the parents'.

the useful with the agreeable! The Emperor showered compliments on the Queen – it was a good thing they were not staying in England for too long, or they would end by forgetting France completely – handed out rings and watches to equerries, pages, and other officials, gave the Master of the Household a bracelet (for his wife), diamond pins to the Clerk Comptroller of the Kitchen and the Clerk of the Stables, and tipped the servants handsomely to the tune of £300. The Empress gave Vicky and Alice each a ring and a bracelet, and the other children lockets containing her hair. The youngest children burst into tears, the band played 'Partant pour la Syrie', and the royal and imperial

Departure of Napoleon and Eugénie from Osborne. Victoria and Albert both agreed, wrote the Queen in her journal for 10 August 1857, 'that the Emperor and Empress had been so particularly amiable . . . for they lived with us as quietly as any other relation.'

standards flew companionably together as Victoria and Albert took their departing guests out to the *Reine Hortense* in a sea '*alive* with vessels'. Guns saluted, the Emperor's band played God Save the Queen, and from the deck of the *Reine Hortense* the Empress kissed her hand, waving her handkerchief over and over again. The French crew shouted 'Vive la Reine d'Angleterre' and the crew of the *Fairy* gave three cheers. And all was over. By the time Victoria and Albert sat down to a belated luncheon the *Reine Hortense* was out of sight.

'Poor dear modest unpretentious Osborne', said the Queen feeling very flat after all the excitement, 'kept its simple character in spite of the distinguished guests.'[86] She congratulated herself that, with the exception of the Ball, a larger dinner table, more carriages and servants, a great many extra police and a large draft of French Secret Police, all had been 'just as usual'.[87]

Dear modest Osborne was still undergoing further embellishments, and the interiors were receiving what were to be Albert's final touches. Late in 1857 the ceiling of the dining room was painted and gilded – 'which looks most lovely'.[88] Two years later the Council Room also was painted and decorated, with oak leaves and laurel leaves, symbols of honour and achievement, to a

design by Ludwig Gruner. Fountains were placed at the Landing House, and planting continued as always, Albert staking out plantations and avenues of Guernsey Elms, *Pinus austriaca* and evergreen oaks all over the estate. The sea cliff was planted with *Cupressus lambertiana*, *Pinus austriaca*, alders, willows, and evergreen oak seedlings, and tamarisk at the back of the sea wall. Stables, piers, cottages, boatsheds, paths, walls, workshops, dog-kennels, a cricket ground, lodges, gates, Albert always had a project in hand. He even began to rebuild Whippingham Church.

More changes, and less pleasant than those imposed on this little kingdom by Albert, were on their way. Vicky was only fourteen when she was promised to Prince Frederick William of Prussia. With small children Albert was a strict, but enlightened parent but as they grew older his handling of them faltered; at about this time he wrote to Vicky: 'To little children the world is particularly indulging, because *one hopes* that they will change, but you are now standing on the threshold of the youthful period of life and that makes me very very anxious.'[89] Vicky's enjoyment of her last few summers at Osborne was sharpened by her sense of the coming separation; she was at the Swiss Cottage on the very morning that her mother was in the Council Room formally declaring the forthcoming marriage. When Vicky left Osborne as an unmarried girl for the last time, at the end of 1857, rather tearful, she was partly consoled by her parents' promise that her garden would ways be kept for her, as in turn were all the children's; they were to remain so, planted out as the children had had them, until 1927.

Vicky married Fritz in January 1858 when she was just seventeen. As a young wife, living in Berlin, she continued to hear about Osborne through the Queen's letters: 'Yesterday there was a grand tea at the Swiss Cottage and imagine good Affie by way of amusement exhibiting his air pump and steam engine (puffing and blowing all the time – in the tool house) to Grandmama, the others and the little Greys – and pumping over himself and Arthur.'[90] Arthur, aged eight, knew just what was most important about that particular afternoon: 'I caught a butterfly at the Swiss Cottage and Affie made there some experiments and I got very wet.'[91]

Such experiments were not the only manly pursuits which occupied Albert's sons at the Swiss Cottage. They extended their practical experience soon after the end of the Crimean War, when Bertie and Affie built a surprise close by for Mama's birthday, a miniature earthworks properly fortified with redoubts, as directed by Lieutenant Cowell of the Royal Engineers, Affie's governor. Four years later Arthur, aged ten, and Leopold, aged six, helped to build a miniature barracks of brick inside the defences of the fort. It was another good opportunity to practise royal duties so Lenchen laid the first stone. Beatrice, aged three, also assisted at the ceremony and seems to have rather irritated her elder brothers with her constant questions.[92] The Queen, passing by, saw how hard the boys worked at it, but it was a lengthy project, not finished until Bastille Day in 1861. Victoria Fort and Albert Barracks, as they were called, with their white paintwork and the white miniature cannon in position can still be seen there today.

The 'dear Swiss Cottage': it was dressed up for high days and holidays, decked with flags for birthdays when balloons and parachutes were let off, and when Vicky came back in 1859 she was welcomed with 'two pretty arches and

Vicky at Osborne, 1855, still a child, but already promised to Prince Frederick William of Prussia. The photograph was taken by J. J. E. Mayall whom the Queen thought 'the oddest man I ever saw, but an excellent photographer. He is an American, and a tremendous enthusiast in his work.' (RA QVJ, 28 July 1855)

The Swiss Cottage
gardens, *c*.1857, decorated
for a celebration.

an inscription'. She had left behind in Berlin her husband and her son William,
so it was quite like old times as she joined in the cookery on Lenchen's birthday.
'She is still quite the *child*, yet with the knowledge of a married woman', wrote
the Queen,[93] relieved that the dark facts of marriage had not rubbed the bloom
off Vicky's youth. When Vicky's second child, Charlotte, was born, the juvenile
uncles and aunts celebrated the arrival of their niece with a supper of their own
cooking at the Swiss Cottage. Victoria and Albert themselves enjoyed the
children's retreat; driving down there one balmy evening with Bertie and Alice
to be joined by Ernest Leiningen, the Queen's nephew who commanded the
royal yacht, and his wife Marie. They had a cold dinner and afterwards, wrote
Victoria, 'walked down to the sea, which was very calm and the night
wonderfully hot, with a brilliant moonshine. We ladies sat for some time on the
top of the Landing House and drove home at a quarter to eleven.'[94]

Before she married, Vicky had played duets with her father; now Alice
stepped into the role of eldest daughter in this and many other ways; when the
Queen had a painting lesson with Leitch these days it was 'quite a class' if Alice

and Lenchen were painting too. In 1859 Alice took part in eight-handed duets on two pianos, with the Queen, Albert, and a member of the Household to make up the fourth: 'Such a noise as we made – and such a mess of it too! generally all playing the same piece, indeed, but at two or three bars interval.'[95] They played in the drawing room, where even the Queen complained of the dreadful cold; Osborne was undoubtedly better suited to summer than to winter, but occasionally the temperate maritime winters turned cold enough to provide the children with fun. Such was the winter of 1859 when in two days sixty cartloads of ice were stored away in the ice house, which since 1853 had sported a grand ornamental doorway. A deep fall of snow followed by bright sunshine infected everyone with good humour. The Prince of Wales and his entourage built a snowman. Even Albert came out to help, though he was these days not so much the carefree young father as the hard-pressed bureaucrat with a strong fellow-feeling for the donkey in Carisbrooke that endlessly turned round in the wheel at the Castle well. A tobogganing party began, with Albert pulling the little sledge himself, and treading down

By the late 1850s, the family circle was beginning to fragment, but most of the children were at Osborne for the Queen's birthday in 1859. From left to right: Leopold, Louise, the Queen, Arthur, Alice, Vicky (now married), Beatrice, Albert, and Lenchen.

the loose snow. After luncheon they all went out again and the Queen watched Albert and the children sliding down the slopes below the terrace on their little sledges. In January 1861 the pond at Barton was thickly frozen over and the sky was still and bright. Alice, Albert, the boys, and the Gentlemen all skated while the Queen watched. As ever, she had eyes only for her husband: 'It was beautiful to see him skimming and sweeping along with such grace and lightness, making the inner and outer curve first on one leg and then on another; in a black velvet jacket.'[96] He had skates with swans on the end of them and this was to be the last time that he ever used them.

The health of the Queen's mother, the Duchess of Kent, had become the cause of grave concern. There had once been difficulties and estrangements between them, but these were all long in the past; now they were in close, daily contact, and when the Duchess died in March 1861, the Queen suffered a nervous collapse. Three weeks later they all embarked for Osborne 'quite privately, no-one there, not a flag, or a gun fired'.[97] The Queen felt very tired, but the next day she went over 'to the room where all the boxes with dearest

OPPOSITE: *Beatrice in a burnous*, by Winterhalter, 1859. She was a bright, mischievous child with a mind of her own, who would sit on Albert's knee at luncheon to sing nursery rhymes and wheedle bits of cake out of him.

Even with Beatrice, her last child, the Queen had not lost the urge to dash off spontaneous sketches or to carefully paint her strawberry-blond hair.

Mama's letters were being unpacked and sorted. There are some such interesting, curious ones.'[98] During the course of the next three weeks, she and Albert sorted through the Duchess's papers, a 'sad but interesting task.'[99] They 'arranged' those letters which they thought were 'valuable and interesting' and burnt the others, including many from the Queen herself.[100] They went through the Duchess's jewellery, dividing it up among her grandchildren; adopted her terrier, Baz, who soon grew accustomed to walking with them; and discussed eternity on the way back from the Swiss Cottage.

The Prince Consort, by Weisall, *c*.1860. For some years Albert had been suffering from chronic low health, not helped by the punishing agenda of work which he set himself to do.

In August, Vicky visited Osborne with her husband Fritz and her two children William and Charlotte, having experienced considerable opposition to the visit in Berlin from the Prussian royal family and their doctors who were not at all happy at the heirs to the house of Hohenzollern being spirited away to the damp and perniciously liberal shores of the Isle of Wight. The young Hohenzollerns held their own. William chased his youngest aunt round and round the Queen's luncheon table – Beatrice was rather afraid of him as he was so violent – and his sister Charlotte looked a very pretty sight when she was brought to the Queen's sitting room and lay in the old cradle which all Victoria and Albert's children, beginning with Alice, had used. William was put into a

OPPOSITE: The Duchess of Kent, by Weisall. Relations between the Queen and her mother had once been strained, but for many years the two had been in friendly, though not intimate, daily contact; her death was the first real bereavement that the Queen experienced.

OPPOSITE: The Queen and Beatrice in mourning for the Duchess of Kent, by H. Krano, 1861.

'Aunt and niece, Beatrice with Charlotte of Prussia', by the Queen, 1861. With such a large family, it soon became difficult to distinguish between the generations.

sailor suit, and the Queen reached for her pen to sketch him, for he looked 'such a duck' in it. Charlotte's first birthday was celebrated in the correct style and her present table was laid out in the breakfast room; Beatrice, Charlotte, and William 'all so smart' and the only ones not wearing black, the royal family still all being in mourning for the Duchess of Kent. The Queen's grandchildren rapidly became 'the best children I ever saw, never shy or put out'.[101] William, the future Kaiser, bogeyman of the Allies in the First World War, was always to enjoy something of a special relationship with his grandmother.

Since Vicky's marriage, she had been drawn into her parents' search for a possible bride for Bertie. The Queen and Prince had originally opposed Vicky's suggestion of the Princess Alexandra of Denmark, but had come to realize that the Danish beauty did in fact meet most of the stringent criteria of politics, religion and personal appearance required to marry the heir to the throne.

The seventeen years difference between Vicky and Beatrice meant that the generations had already begun to elide; one moment the Queen and Vicky were walking down to the Swiss Cottage plotting how Bertie could 'accident- ally' meet his princess; the next they were laughing at the droll antics of the smallest children and sitting down to tea to relish what the other children had produced that morning in the porcelain kitchen. With laughter and plans for the future the Queen's grief for her mother was beginning to heal naturally, but she had not yet fully recovered when she was dealt a far more grievous blow.

Aunt & niece, Beatrice with Charlotte of Prussia

July 22. 186

CHAPTER SIX

DEAR DESOLATE OSBORNE

Albert never had the magnificent constitution of his wife. She bore him nine live children and concealed in her small body a prodigious strength. The Queen realized that he, on the other hand, was not strong, and it made her anxious. For years he suffered from a temperamental digestion, from 'rheumatism', from painful inflamed gums. He overworked himself, and drove his children hard. The strenuous programme he mapped out for them was no more than he himself had undergone as a boy. It suited the Princess Royal, who responded to the same intellectual stimulus as her father, but had the opposite effect on the Prince of Wales. It was Bertie's lasting misfortune, as far as relations with his mother were concerned, that his father, at a point when he was far from well, discovered that Bertie had slept with an actress. Albert, already worn out with overwork and chronic low health, was deeply affected. Not only did he see it as a moral disaster for his son, but he also feared that any scandal might jeopardize Bertie's prospects with Princess Alexandra. The Prince Consort travelled to Cambridge to see his son, to make him understand the enormity of what he had done, and returned with the seeds of death already in him.

Albert is commonly supposed to have died of typhoid; retrospective diagnoses have suggested that for some time he had been suffering from cancer of the liver, or stomach. Several people close to him saw that the man who had worked so hard for his Queen and his adopted country did not have the will to fight for himself. After several weeks of fever, during which he continued to work without sparing himself, Albert died in the Blue Room at Windsor Castle on 14 December 1861, with Victoria at his side.

Within a few days of this 'dreadful and overwhelming calamity', even as Albert's funeral arrangements were being made by Messrs Dowbiggin and Sons, the same firm that had supplied the original furniture for Osborne, the

When Albert died, the Queen's life shattered. He had disliked effigies, but almost immediately she determined that memorials to him would be 'numberless'. Here, his bust is surrounded by his daughters. From left to right: Alice, Lenchen, Beatrice, Vicky, and Louise; photograph by William Bambridge, March 1862.

Queen had reluctantly left Windsor, where the panoply of death made such a horrible contrast to the usual Christmas decorations, and had shut herself away to grieve in the small, friendly rooms in the house where Albert had always been happiest and which she loved for his sake. 'The whole house seems to have lost its Light, its *very soul*', wrote Queen Victoria at Osborne in the bitter, desolate January of 1862, three weeks after Albert's death.[1]

Here she could nurse the mortal wound which she felt had split her in two: '*Can* I – *can* I be alive when half my body and soul are gone?'[2] She was mourning not just her husband, but the man who had been everything to her, 'father, mother, friend, companion, advisor, lover, guardian angel'.[3] Without him, she felt utterly lost:

He did everything – everywhere! *Nothing* did I do – without him – from the greatest to the smallest – from State Affairs – from Political Questions to the arranging [of] our Albums, our little photographs, the designing and ordering of Jewelry, the buying of a dress or a bonnet . . . *all* was done together; my first word was 'I must ask Albert'.[4]

At its most basic, practical level, she had also lost an invaluable private secretary; and she now found herself overwhelmed with papers: 'So much to do, so many boxes, letters, – business';[5] and no Albert to read, explain, advise, draft, clarify. Victoria faced the despatch boxes alone; 'so careful and nervously anxious to do the right thing, feeling so forlorn without beloved Albert'.[6]

She was completely at the mercy of her grief, and would wake in the mornings 'with a dreamy, dreadful confusion of something having happened and crushed me! Oh! it is too awful, too dreadful! And a sickness and icy coldness bordering on the wildest despair comes over me – which is more than a human being can bear.'[7] She fell prey to terrible sick headaches; the slightest noise, so much as the rustle of a gown, could set her nerves on edge and a hush fell over the house which seemed to one visitor 'like Pompeii, the life suddenly extinguished'.[8]

The Court went about with thin, careworn faces, the Queen kept to her rooms and saw no one but her children and a very few others. Everyone was plunged into black: Queen, children, Household. The women on the estate, fifty-two of them, were each issued with yards of black material to make themselves dresses, a long 'scarf shawl' and four yards of black ribbon.

Nothing was too small for an image of the 'beloved Angel'. This memorial ring in gold and black enamel contains a micro-photograph of Albert in 1861 (attributed to J. J. E. Mayall).

For the rest of her life, the Queen's letters were written on paper with deep black edges.

The house itself, which had recently been undergoing more decoration inside, with gilding on the staircase in the Pavilion, plasterwork pilasters and panels in corridors and plaster festoons over doors, now received the gloomiest ornament of all, a hatchment. This was a funeral escutcheon or armorial shield carved in wood, enclosed in a black diamond-shaped frame, which it was customary to hang up on a deceased person's house over the entrance at the level of the second floor. Normally it stayed up for six to twelve months and was then taken to the parish church.

The lonely Queen and Beatrice, photograph by Ghemar Frères, c.1862. The child's affectionate ways did not comfort the young widow, but only made her sadder.

The royal children had to cope with their own grief and support their inconsolable mother. It was not easy; even Beatrice's childish demonstrations of affection, which it had been hoped would help to comfort the Queen only upset her. One of the few who brought the Queen comfort was her Poet Laureate, Alfred Tennyson. She was soothed and pleased by his melodious requiem for a much-loved friend who had drowned, and was sure that 'Only those who have suffered, as I do, can understand these beautiful poems.'[9] *In Memoriam* returned a faithful echo:

> Still onwards winds the dreary way;
> I with it; for I long to prove
> No lapse of moons can canker love,
> Whatever fickle tongues may say.

Uncle Leopold came over from Belgium and stayed at Osborne for several weeks; when he left, Vicky arrived from Berlin: but the chief burden fell on Alice, now a willowy eighteen. She slept in the Queen's room, where her mother slept like a penitent in a 'wretched little bed' at the foot of the great bed she had used before Albert's death.[10] It was Alice who drove Victoria out for soothing fresh air in the Sardinian pony carriage which, because it ran smoothly and silently on rubber wheels, did not aggravate the Queen's constant headaches, and it was Alice who accompanied the Queen on her daily visits to the colony of artists already in residence at Osborne, working on sketches, ideas, and casts for a variety of effigies.

Queen Victoria valued objects for their associations. Lockets of hair, pictures, paintings, photographs of dear ones, and now especially, representations of her dear dead husband. Mr Theed's bust was 'admirable' – it 'positively seems to smile'[11] – but his statue of Albert in Highland dress required 'a good deal of alteration'; the Queen and Alice helped him in 'improving the figure'. Marochetti, whose work was so familiar from the birthday tables, bowed to royal taste and 'at once' adopted Vicky's ideas for the

The Queen's bedroom, photograph by Jabez Hughes, 1875. Pinned to the bedhead is a wreath and a picture of Albert on his deathbed.

recumbent statue for the mausoleum at Frogmore. Mr Say pleased the Queen greatly with his representation of Albert in a suit of allegorical armour, while the tinted eyes in the photograph which Mr Harrack had coloured 'quite look at me', said the Queen, 'as if to tell me what to do!'[12] If the truth be known, the eyes told the Queen only what she wanted to hear, for already she was going her own way in Albert's name. He himself had disliked statues and effigies but the Queen had already decided that his memorials and images would be 'numberless'. She pursued her objective with such energy that it was not long before one of her more famous subjects, Charles Dickens, was driven to beseech a remote friend: 'If you should meet with an inaccessible cave anywhere in that neighbourhood, to which a hermit could retire from the memory of Prince

Albert and testimonials to the same, pray let me know of it. We have nothing solitary and deep enough in this part of England.'[13]

There could be no better memorial to 'former happy times' than the house which was so completely Albert's creation. Athough the Queen felt that her own life was from now on to be 'day turned into night', the house and all that it contained must remain as Albert had made it; nothing must be changed. She considered putting a clause into her new will to prevent her heirs from changing Albert's arrangements either. For the rest of the Queen's life her obsession kept the interiors as Albert had left them: happiness preserved in the resinous tears of a grief that in time solidified into habit.

Albert's room, in particular, must remain as though he had just walked out

Albert's creation became his memorial and for years remained as he had designed it, until the Queen plucked up courage to make minor additions, being, she said, 'so afraid to meddle with or spoil what the dear Prince had planned and built.'
(RA PP Osb. 539)

of it, or rather, as though he might just walk into it. In the initial months of her grief the Queen spent much of her time in there; it became breakfast room, Council Room, birthday and writing room, after-dinner sitting room, and audience chamber: the scene of tearful encounters, on both sides, with those who were meeting Victoria for the first time as a widow. She looked, said one, 'sadly worn and thinned, and very small altogether, in her little widow's cap, without strings but with streamers behind, and her heavy clinging woollen gown.'[14] She talked about Albert as though he was in the next room, and indeed visitors expected him to walk in any moment, for the Prince's wash-hand stand and things were all arranged as though ready for him, his pen and blotting book were laid out on his writing table, his handkerchief lay on the sofa, his watch was going and there were fresh flowers in the glass; everything was just as it had always been – '*all* remains the same', insisted Her Majesty.

A large house and estate demands constant attention and upkeep. When the house had to be redecorated, it was done with the old colours and patterns, which made life difficult for the Queen's Clerk of the Works. The chintz-patterned wallpapers sprawling with fat roses went out of fashion and were no longer kept in stock. They had to be specially printed, which was expensive in such small quantities, and if the copy did not match exactly the old paper, even if it was for a governess's bedroom, the Clerk of the Works hesitated to hang it, preferring to keep it for papering servants' rooms.[15] As patterns went out of date, contemporary eyes perceived 'the oddest combinations of upholstery'.

The Queen had to address some signs that the rest of the world had not ceased to exist with Albert. The trees in the pleasure grounds and woods continued to grow, necessitating decisions: 'I did not attend to many things when out with him,' sighed the Queen regretfully, 'which would be so useful to me now – about trees and planting and plans of his.'[16] Andrew Toward, faithful steward since the very beginning, knew much about what Albert had intended; the Queen consulted him before deciding what should be done, got him to teach her some of their names, and continued to take a dutiful interest in learning, thinning, pruning, and planting, though never with the knowledgeable pleasure and pride that Albert had felt. Toward's awareness of what Albert wished was a precious link with her lost husband. Hitherto Albert had dealt with estate business, but after 1861 Victoria saw more of her steward; if a wet spell caused a landslide on the bank by the sea, if there was a question about how to proceed with the unfinished Landing House, or new farm buildings, if trees which Albert had intended should be thinned needed to be marked for felling, the widow braced herself to go down to the spot and see Toward about it. She could quite easily have delegated any of these tasks, but she wished to continue as before, with Osborne now entirely under her personal control.

After Albert's death, the farm no longer kept up to date lacking the guiding presence of an innovative mind interested in the latest technology. The Queen's sentimental interest in it hampered rather than helped the duties of the ageing Land Steward. There was, for instance, the matter of the rabbits. Albert would not allow a single one on the place;[17] the Queen, on the other hand, wished their numbers should be 'kept down but not entirely destroyed', though rats must be '*exterminated*'.[18] Consequently rabbits became a chronic problem and did serious damage, but the gamekeepers and the tenant farmers were not allowed to shoot them and must not use their nets or traps when the Queen was in residence, as she feared her dogs might be injured.

The children's collections in their museum at the Swiss Cottage continued to grow. It had been Albert's intention to put up another building to house it, so the Queen reluctantly complied, and inspected the cases with Alice to decide which should be taken down and placed in the new building; 'It made me so sad and wretched, for I cannot bear any change, though I know dearest Albert wished this to be done. Every little thing he had worked at and planned out, reminds me so terribly of former happy days and makes me sick at heart.'[19]

The most pressing of all demonstrations that time was moving on was that '*our*' children were growing. The Queen was determined that 'dear customs' should be kept up,[20] so on Maundy Thursday Beatrice brought her basket of

The interiors remained as the Prince had designed them. When they needed redecorating, the old colours were carefully matched and when the Queen acquired new pictures, she went to great pains to hang them without disturbing Albert's arrangement.

coloured eggs in while the Queen was breakfasting and Alice and Affie hid them
for the youngest children. The childrens' rites of passage were very painful to
the Queen without Albert and she had to steel herself to greet them – in Albert's
room – to wish them happy birthday and to bring them through to show them
their present tables laid out in her sitting room; or listen to them   in Albert's
room – be examined before their confirmation in Whippingham Church, and
after the service give them – in Albert's room – their presents of jewellery and
the family order which she had decided to establish called the Victoria and
Albert Order.

The first family event of note to take place after Albert's death was Alice's
wedding. The Queen's second daughter had not had a bright start to grown-up
life. Her engagement to Prince Louis of Hesse had been overshadowed by the
death of the Duchess of Kent, which precluded any celebrations; on a visit to
Osborne in 1861 her fiancé had most unromantically caught measles from her
younger brothers and sisters; and now her wedding was blighted by Albert's
death, postponed by the death of an aunt in the house of Hesse, and plunged at
the last moment into, if possible, even blacker gloom, by the death of Bertie's
governor, General Bruce. Poor Alice's wedding was described by the Queen as
'more like a funeral than a wedding',[21] not without a note of satisfaction in her
tone: this was just as it should be now that Albert was no more.

Alice and Louis were eventually united in the dining room at Osborne on
Tuesday, 1 July 1862. Only Louis's immediate family and a handful of the
Queen's relations had been invited, but they were of course, all royalty, so each
came with a retinue; Osborne House and the surrounding cottages overflowed.

OPPOSITE: *Princess Alice*, by
Winterhalter, 1861. As
eldest unmarried daughter
at the time of Albert's
death, she shouldered the
heavy burden of
supporting the stricken
Queen.

*Marriage of Princess Alice to
Prince Louis of Hesse*, by
Thomas, 1862. The
ceremony was held in the
dining room at Osborne
under the 'Family Picture'.
The Queen had to struggle
to keep her composure, but
was sure that the painted
hand of Prince Albert was
reaching out with his
blessing.

The Queen kept as quiet as ever: 'all this bustle going on, with my heart utterly broken and my nerves so shattered, is very trying.'[22]

The ceremonies were arranged in such a way as to emphasize rather than ease the family's bereavement. A few nights before the wedding, Alice moved out of her rooms to Albert's room, and to sleep with the Queen. It was in Albert's room that the Queen gave Alice and Louis the wedding presents of jewellery which she and Albert had prepared for Alice and the silver which she had chosen alone for Louis; and on the morning of the wedding, it was in Albert's room that Alice put on her wedding dress. The Queen was alive to the horrible reality: 'She (Alice) is dressing in her *Beloved Papa's* room, while *I* am having my widow's cap adjusted! I think it is a dreadful dream!'[23] Furthermore, Alice was married at an altar placed directly under the 'Family Picture'; the contrast between the 'former happy times' represented in the painting and the miserable present was certainly deliberate – had the Queen so wished, the ceremony could just as easily have taken place in the Council Room or the drawing room, either of which would have been big enough for the occasion.

The ladies-in-waiting began the day wearing black, changed for the ceremony into the colours of half-mourning, grey and lilac ('it was quite odd to me', said one, 'to be in light colours again'[24]), and almost all plunged into black again immediately afterwards. Alice's trousseau was black, but on her wedding day at least she was permitted to wear white. Her wedding dress had the graceful flowing skirts fashionable in the early 1860s, a deep flounce of Honiton lace, and sprigs of myrtle and orange blossom around the hem; the bodice was cut 'half-high'. She shielded her maiden blushes with a veil, also of Honiton lace, and wore a wreath of orange blossoms and myrtle. She had no train. Her jewellery consisted of the family order and an opal cross and brooch. Her bridesmaids, Lenchen, Louise, Beatrice, and Louis's sister, Princess Anna of Hesse, wore sprigged net over white, with mauve trimmings. The Queen, it goes without saying, trembled through this emotional day in her widow's weeds.

'It was *very solemn – very affecting, very sad*', wrote Victoria after the ceremony.[25] The painted Albert in the Family Picture stretched out his hand just as if to bless his daughter; the archbishop, with the tears streaming down his face, 'read the service (bereft of its worst coarsenesses) beautifully! But', the Queen went on, 'when it came to the words *till death us do part* I could not restrain my tears – tho' I struggled and I did command myself till all was over. Affie sobbed dreadfully all through.'[26]

They signed the register in the Horn Room and then the Queen took leave of the guests and went upstairs, where she was joined for lunch by Alice and Louis. The visiting royalties ate their wedding breakfast in the Council Room, their suites were consigned to a tent on the lawn. After lunch Alice sat to Mr Thomas for a 'slight sketch', for the painting he was doing of the ceremony. Then she went into Albert's room to change her dress, putting on a white *mousseline de soie* with a little bonnet trimmed with orange blossoms. As the bride left for her honeymoon, her mother gave her a few parting words of advice on married life and assured her that although she might be apprehensive, 'all was God's will and she was safe with her husband!'[27]

The 'honey couple' drove away from Osborne in a chariot and four, the carriage servants in plain liveries (festive scarlet or epaulette liveries being unthinkable at a time like this), to St Clare at Ryde. They spent the following day there, quite alone except for two gentlemen and one lady-in-waiting and a houseful of servants, and the day after that the Queen came over in the afternoon to see how they were getting on. Alice had rather a cold, but was 'very quiet and posée'. The Queen looked at her daughter closely: 'Oh! how strange it is – to see one's dear innocent child in one day become a woman, with all the

The bedroom which was used by Alice and Louis after their marriage. Visitors to Osborne were made very comfortable and were struck by the care and attention to detail.

knowledge of her mother . . . God bless her! She said she would have been very much alarmed but *then* she recollected my parting words, – and *all* was right!'[28]

Alice and Louis were allowed another day at St Clare, before returning to Osborne, where Alice's duties included reading to the Queen from Tennyson's 'The Lady of Shalott', a poem as rich and sombre as a stained glass window, quite in keeping with the tenebrous atmosphere of Osborne. The corpse of beauty floated down the river towards forbidden Camelot:

> And in the lighted palace near
> Died the sound of royal cheer;
> And they crossed themselves for fear

It must have been a relief for Alice, in spite of her tears at parting, when a week after her wedding she left Osborne and her childhood behind and sailed for her new home in Hesse-Darmstadt. The Queen could not bear to watch her daughter go and deliberately created a diversion for herself, so that when she came up to her room, the yacht was gone from the bay below. But however 'dear and precious' Alice had been as a comfort and assistance, the Queen soon confessed with cruel candour, 'I hardly miss her at all, or felt her going, – so *utterly* absorbed am I by that *one* dreadful loss.'[29]

Andrew Toward with his son Tommy, photograph by Dr E. Becker, 21 August 1854. The Land Steward had worked at Osborne from the very beginning and for the widowed Queen his knowledge of Albert's plans were a precious link with the past.

She still, however, had to address herself to the problem of Bertie. His marriage to Alix, as she was known in her family, had now become for the Queen 'a sacred duty he, our darling Angel, left us to perform.'[30] Alix accepted Bertie, and with her father came to stay at Osborne in November 1862. Blue lights were burning on the ships in the Bay, and the music from the band aboard the *Emerald* drifted across the calm water. As the waves broke along the shore they shone like silver in the moonlight, and two excited representatives of the family, Lenchen and Leopold, waited impatiently at the landing place to receive her, longing to get out of the carriage and stand on the wet stones, only restrained by the lady-in-waiting with them. Up in the house dinner was delayed (Alix came to be notorious for her unpunctuality) and the Queen stayed her hunger with a bowl of soup. Victoria welcomed the beautiful Alix as another daughter, decided she was loveable, gentle and good, permitted a wintery 'gleam of satisfaction' to shine into her heart, and allowed herself to see Alix as a jewel come from another world to brighten this dreary mortal path.

Nevertheless the hatchment still hung over the door. Bertie and Alix used Osborne for their honeymoon in 1863 and naturally Bertie wanted this melancholy escutcheon, which had already been there longer than was customary, to be taken down. But this was a sensitive area. The Queen blamed her son for precipitating the illness which had killed Albert, so Bertie had to be careful not to give the impression that he was trying to hasten the obsequies which were justly due to his father's memory and a certain amount of tactful manoeuvring was necessary. He had the support of the Queen's Household; the Woman of the Bedchamber wrote to the Master of the Household:

I spoke to the Queen last evening about the hatchment being up during the honeymoon without alluding to the Prince of Wales' own wish about it. – But said it never was done, as it was considered so ill-omened and unlucky – the Queen said *at first* she could not have it taken down – but was evidently uneasy at the notion of its being thought ominous. If she speaks to you please back me up– and say that it will be thought very unlucky – without alluding to what the Prince of Wales said himself.[31]

The hatchment did come down for the duration of the honeymoon, Bertie and Alix enjoyed a few days of 'perfect bliss' as 'happiest of women and most fortunate of men', but after they had left, it was put back again exactly as before. It left a permanent mark on the stucco, still visible twenty years later, a ghostly echo of the dreadful void in the Queen's life.

Horse-drawn lawn mower, 1897; it used to take fourteen days to mow all the lawns.

Other than looking at pictures and busts of the dear departed, or talking about him and eternity, it was hard to know how to console the Queen. If Osborne looked desolate, it was because Albert was not there; if it looked sunny and bright with flowers, that was almost worse because it reminded her of how happy they had been and how miserably wretched she now was. The trees and shrubs that she saw from her writing table, placed in the window of Albert's room, reminded her how fond of them he had been; the Mediterranean heath in bloom on the terrace brought back all Albert's joy when he could escape from the bustle and fatigue of London; moonlit walks on the terrace only made her inexpressibly sad. When she heard the nightingales, she wept for Albert. When she sat in the alcove every descending step she heard was his. The music ('*poor music* – it will never be touched again very likely'[32]) lay silent by the pianos, the Journey Albums were closed 'for ever'. She would never wear a low dress again; no one would ever see her shoulders because he was no longer there to admire them. Sundays at Osborne were now the most trying days because they had once been the happiest.

She expressed the dislocation in her life by her altered use of the rooms at Osborne. Albert's room, as we have seen, became a focus for family ceremonies, and in the very early days of 'my misery' she used it as a Council Room too; everything was 'well and kindly arranged' to accommodate her complete seclusion, with the Councillors in Albert's room, and she in her sitting room with the door open. The business was all summed up in two paragraphs and the Clerks of the Council read out the 'approved' for her; technically she had held a Council, but her Privy Councillors had neither seen nor heard her. She avoided sitting in the drawing room after dinner, and just as she could not face the Council Room for Councils, she would not use the dining room to eat in. For nearly two years after Albert died she dined in the Horn Room or the Council Room. When eventually she braved the dining room it was, she declared, 'a great struggle and effort, but I longed to be back again there. Sat in the place where my darling used to.'[33]

She also altered the timing of her visits, for her calendar had now become a minefield of anniversaries, and she picked her way through the year avoiding the most painful conjunctions. She no longer came to Osborne for her once-happy birthday, nor for Albert's. She spent the dreadful 14 December, anniversary of Albert's death, at Windsor, and then went to Osborne for Christmas, Windsor being too closely associated with Albert's special festival.

Queen Victoria set a sober routine for Christmas at Osborne. In the drawing room the Sèvres vases on either side of the statue of the infant Beatrice were filled with Christmas holly, yew, and ferns; the bust of the Prince Consort in the hall was decorated with holly and ivy, and the pillars of Whippingham Church wreathed with similar greenery. Presents, nicely graded according to the rank and station of the recipients, were given out, following the German custom, on Christmas Eve. Before luncheon the Queen gave her maids and personal servants theirs; and late in the afternoon went down to the servants' hall in the basement with the ladies and gentlemen of the Household for the tenants' Christmas tree, in some years to give meat or plum pudding to the labourers and blankets or flannel petticoats to their wives, and in other years to give material for dresses or trousers, toys, books, and cake to their children, who also received the ornaments cut off the tree. Then which ever of the Queen's children were in the house would give the Ladies and Gentlemen their presents and lastly, the Queen and her family had their own Christmas tree in the dining room.

A tragic and moving inscription in one of the Queen's pocket sketch books. She had always prayed that she would not survive Albert; she outlived him by forty years.

The ceremony at the royal tree was now a subdued occasion. In Albert's day, the present room, with its tree and a present table for each member of the family, would remain laid out until Twelfth Night; now the candles on the tree were lit for the last time on Christmas Day and the presents were taken away. She gave her children jewellery, ornaments, books, dresses, and furs. The first Christmas that the Queen celebrated at Osborne there were two little pictures for her from Albert, which he had bought in Brussels in 1860. They were waiting for her under the dear Family Picture. Such gifts, 'so precious and so sad',[34] set the Queen quite a puzzle, for how and where was she to hang them without disturbing any of dearest Albert's arrangements? The first few times the Queen went about the house placing new pictures, she took Alice, who was visiting, with her; 'terribly sad and trying' she found it too, 'as I am always missing *the* one who had the right taste.'[35] Albert had never done much to give the Queen confidence in her own judgement in this field, as she fondly recalled: '*How* often he used to laugh at my *want* of artistic taste.'[36]

Slowly, very slowly, the Queen began to recover. She ceased to refer to 'our' children; gradually they became 'my' children. On her wedding anniversary, now always spent at Osborne, she gave thanks for the happiness she had once had. She began to respond to attempts to cheer her up, and could

The Queen thought that spinning might be a soothing occupation for a lonely young widow, and had a spinning wheel in her sitting room. Drawing by Sir Joseph Boehm, 1869.

listen with relative equanimity to her daughters playing compositions by Albert on his harmonium, and even music that was not by him such as hits from Gounod's *Faust*. Once, to her own astonishment, she even sang – but only for a moment. In summer Alice and Lenchen persuaded her to go out on the water in a rowing boat as they thought it might be good for her. In the winter of 1864 John Brown, one of the ghillies from Balmoral, was brought to Osborne and the Queen took up riding again, given confidence by the dependable Scottish presence at her pony's head. As ever, the shade of Albert walked alongside them: 'I find this quiet riding, in these dear grounds, woods, and fields by the sea, very pleasant, and the motion of the pony's gentle walk, soothing. But it is a sad alternative for the delightful long walks with my beloved one.'[37]

Princess Beatrice and Dacko, by Landseer, 1865.

It was not long before Brown made himself indispensable, and the Queen had decided that he should remain with her permanently and make himself useful in other ways besides leading her pony. In John Brown the Queen had found a strong arm to lean on now that Albert had gone. In a crisis he was 'most useful, calm quick and strong',[38] and his brusque manner, couched in the rugged accents of the Highlander – the famous 'Hoots, then, wumman, can ye no hold yerr head up?'[39] having pricked her chin as he fastened her cape for a drive – was an invigorating contrast to the silken deference of the Court, where nowadays there was no one in a position to approach her and forget that she was Queen, and operated wonderfully on the 'luxury of woe' in which she had wrapped herself. She promoted him in rank and salary, marking his rise in her esteem from the status of favoured ghillie to that of trusted friend and servant. Favourites are always disliked, and John Brown, whose privileged position offended against the laws of heirarchy, was no exception; his blunt ways, made

no more courtly by his weakness for the whisky bottle, held no charms for the Queen's family or Court. Society began to whisper; the Queen remained oblivious and shut away, while rumour grew fat on speculation.

As the Queen took to riding again Beatrice was also learning the art, and when the Queen went down to the stables one morning she found her daughter sitting to Sir Edwin Landseer for a painting of her on her pony, Donald. The Queen was siezed with enthusiasm for the sketch he had done, and suddenly saw before her another opportunity to contrast the happy past with the miserable present. Sir Edwin must do two chalk sketches, one of Albert at Balmoral, 'Monarch of the Glen' as it were, having just shot a stag, and the Queen eagerly coming up to have a look at it; then another, the 'reverse of that bright happy time, I as I am now, sad and lonely, seated on my pony, led by Brown, with a representation of Osborne and a dedication telling the present sad truth.'[40] Sir Edwin professed himself delighted with the idea, though he

Sorrow, by Landseer, 1865. When the painting was shown at the Royal Academy in 1867, it fuelled wild, unfounded speculation about the Queen and John Brown. Her long seclusion was damaging to the monarchy and threatened to undermine the work Albert had contributed to making the Hanoverian legacy respectable.

must have anticipated a new bulge in the file he kept called *Royal Fusseries*, and two days later Her Majesty went down to the stables to be photographed with Brown and her pony Flora, 'three times, and very successfully'.[41]

The pastel sketch followed closely the grouping in the photograph; though Landseer glamorized the Queen's pony and hid John Brown's well-worn brogues behind a dachshund. Louise and Lenchen, in their lilac half-mourning are reading on one of the granite seats in front of Osborne, waiting while the Queen finishes reading the despatch which has interrupted their outing. It is a day-to-day scene which would have been familiar to anyone at Osborne at this time. Landseer also painted a version in oils, to hang in the Royal Academy in 1867, and which eventually found its way to the Horn Room, where it hung until the Queen's death, when it was taken away from Osborne, like so much else. It was returned to the Horn Room in 1989. Although Landseer changed the figure of John Brown so that he no longer appeared to be whispering into the ear of the Queen's pony the figure of the controversial Highlander still dwarfed the two Princesses and his attitude held enough proprietorial assurance to shock public opinion, which did not know whether to consider itself scandalized or draw a disapproving veil. Likenesses and images of the Queen were still strictly controlled and the English found it a disagreeable novelty to see the woman whose image they jingled in their pockets and stuck on their letters portrayed in a domestic, intimate setting with the man at the centre of a fever of speculation. 'All is black that is not Brown', concluded satirists and public alike.

The lurid imaginings of the public were far from the truth. Queen Victoria was not mad, or married to John Brown, or in touch with her dead husband through the Highlander's second sight; it was simply that her gaze was firmly fixed on Albert to the exclusion of almost everything else, and quite regardless of appearances. On their wedding anniversary she would wear the gifts he had given her, the sapphire brooch which had been his wedding gift, and the bracelet which he had given her on the last anniversary they had had together. *Sorrow* was as much a memorial to her relationship with her husband as were these mementoes at her neck and wrist, or the monument which Mr Theed and Mr Humbert were putting up for her in Whippingham Church.

She was still looking over her shoulder, as it were, for approval. In the winter of 1864 while at Osborne she listened to a series of lectures, by Max Müller on the origins of language, Professor Tyndale on chemistry and electricity and Professor Hoffmann on atmosphere, air and oxygen, nitrogen and hydrogen. This last took place in the servants' hall, probably because during his demonstrations 'the sparks flew about in the most wonderful manner'.[42] The Queen was interested, but these lectures were an uncharacteristic departure, and were more a dutiful exercise in subjects that would have pleased Albert rather than pursuits she was interested in for their own sake.

When Queen Victoria looked at her children and grandchildren, Albert was with her, in a way which must have given them an extra burden of inferiority, for she made it quite clear that none of them matched up to him. 'I was so proud', she said, remembering past birthdays, 'at seeing the handsome, clever son, with his still handsomer, cleverer father.'[43] Lenchen, Louise, Arthur, Leopold and Beatrice continued to celebrate their own birthdays, and those of members of the family who were not with them at Osborne, with a tea or supper at the Swiss Cottage 'just as dearest Albert would have wished and liked'.[44] When Victoria laughed at a fat, curly-haired granddaughter, she could not help imagining how Albert would have played with her and carried her about. The generations blurred pleasantly when there were toddlers in the nursery overhead and stumbling round the dining room table: 'it seems quite like old times over again and as if they were *our own* children.'[45] Inevitably, some of the children's life and vigour rubbed off on the Queen. They persuaded her down to the Council Room to see the rehearsal, though not the performance, of a play which Arthur and Leopold were acting, Arthur she thought, looking 'wonderful' in a wig with black eyebrows. They diverted her on other occasions, too. Early in 1866, when one of the Queen's relations was nearing the time of her confinement and looking 'a terrible bundle', Arthur remarked at lunch one day that he had never known anyone wear such ugly crinolines, 'they tucked up so'. His mother explained that Marie Leiningen was expecting 'an addition'. 'What for?', asked Arthur. The Queen was amused, and repeated the story, but this was the kind of exchange which made people purse their lips and say that the Queen and royal family were altogether too free and easy in their ways.[46]

Gradually Victoria picked up the threads of old habits. She was sketching again, grandchildren replacing her own children as subjects, and took lessons from Leitch as she had done in the old days. She also, under the aegis of her most talented daughter, Louise, began to paint flowers, 'in quite a new way, using body colour, on brown packing paper'.[47] She tackled various Osborne specialities: snowdrops, rhododendrons, and magnolia buds. There began to be muted entertainments in the Council Room after dinner. The repertoire invariably included selections from Shakespeare – *As You Like It*, the *Merchant of Venice*, or for a special frisson the sleepwalking scene from *Macbeth* – and there would also be readings from favourite poets, such as Longfellow, Southey, Campbell and Tennyson, performed by actors and actresses like Mr and Mrs Alfred Wigan, Mrs Parks, and Mrs Scott Siddons the great granddaughter of Sarah Siddons. Prestigious as these evenings were for the performers, they were a sober page in the history of the likes of Mrs Wigan, who had started her professional career as a rope dancer and performer on stilts.

The Queen began to enjoy music again. In December 1866 the pianist Charles Hallé was summoned to play before her, but this was no elegant drawing-room concert such as she had enjoyed with Albert, for the Queen was dipping her toes cautiously in the waters of pleasure: she and her children listened to Hallé in the seclusion of the schoolroom. His choice of pieces by Beethoven, Heller, and Mendelssohn had its inevitable effect upon her: 'It made me sad', she said, 'particularly the Beethoven and Mendelssohn pieces

New Year card with a photograph of the Queen and Sharp, by W. and D. Downey, *c*.1867.

which my beloved Albert loved so much and we used to play together,'[48] but the experience was more pleasure than pain, for she repeated it the next day, suggesting many of the pieces, and Hallé ceased to worry about his choice, playing what suited him. He was by his own account a great success with the royal family.[49] The Queen took 'most kindly' to music; Lenchen summoned him to her room to play duets with her, and Leopold, the most musical of Albert's sons, bore him away to his room where, said the pianist, 'we were as jolly as two larks'. He was in the middle of a busy season of rehearsals, and wondered how he was to get away from Osborne, writing home that 'the Queen speaks, and Princess Helena speaks as if I were going to stop here for ever'. The rehearsals were hurriedly rearranged, for Hallé had a shrewd eye on the future and forecast quite correctly, that this was 'a visit which the Queen is sure not to forget, and it will keep me in her good graces for ever'. He was often called back to play at Osborne again.

Also staying at Osborne at the time of Hallé's visit was the seven-year-old Prince William of Prussia, and the pianist witnessed quite a battle of wills between two imperious characters. The Queen wanted her grandson to make Hallé a bow, but the prince was 'too shy and resisted, so she asked him what his mama would say if she heard he was so impolite, but this had no effect; she,

Prince William of Prussia, the future Kaiser, on board the *Fairy*, 6 August 1864, by the Queen. She found that her grandchildren were a new source of pleasure.

however, insisted upon it, so at last he looked at her and said "No, I won't." And then it became a hard struggle between them until he gave in, drew himself up, and made me a deep bow.'[50] The Queen's children laughed, and Hallé chose to see the scene as a charming one, but William's grandmother was one of the few people who could bend his pride.

In the same year, Lenchen had married Prince Christian of Schleswig-Holstein at Windsor. They spent their honeymoon at Osborne – that is, they were alone there for two days before being joined by the Queen. When the time came for the couple to leave, the Queen showed that she had come some way since Alice's departure: when this daughter left, the second to set sail from Osborne into the uncharted seas of marriage, the Queen felt equal to watching her go, partly because she knew Lenchen was to live in England and partly because she was regaining some of her lost equilibrium. She stood at her window, 'gazing at the blue sea and the yacht, which was at its old moorings. Watched the boat nearing her, and felt very sad and lonely at heart ... soon the yacht was under weigh and moved off straight across to France.'[51] Now it was Louise's turn to take over the duties of eldest daughter, until she married the Marquess of Lorne, later Duke of Argyll, at Windsor in 1871, leaving the burden of companionship to the Queen's 'last little treasure', Beatrice.

The younger generation takes the air; Affie and Arthur's children at Osborne, 1884. From left to right: Prince Alfred of Edinburgh; Prince Arthur and Princess Margaret of Connaught; Princess Marie, Princess Alexandra and Princess Victoria Melita of Edinburgh. Photograph by Jabez Hughes.

CHAPTER SEVEN

A NEW PAGE

In the years after Albert's death, Queen Victoria always had a daughter or two near at hand, to call upon for companionship. The elder daughters had each in turn shouldered this burden for a while before marrying and leaving home; but the Queen expected her youngest, Beatrice, to remain at her side to the end. The mischievous child grew up in the shadow of a powerful atmosphere of brooding melancholy and grief; the Queen was dominant by position and inclination, and the bright four-year-old who had delighted her father with her forthright ways developed into a young woman so painfully shy that people dreaded sitting next to her at dinner. Difficult conversations were not all her fault, though; there were so many subjects which they must not broach; for instance, the Queen did not wish marriage or weddings to be discussed in front of Beatrice. She reached the age of twenty-one still single, and celebrated her birthday at Osborne; the band playing under her window and the present table in Albert's room inevitably reminded the Queen of 'former happy days'. Arthur came over from Dublin where he was stationed and a little impromptu dance had materialized in the drawing room the day before. They had five dances and the Queen herself danced a quadrille and a waltz with Arthur. She was pleasantly surprised to find that, although she had not danced the waltz in the eighteen years since Albert's death, she could do it as well as ever. In the iron-bound routine of the Queen's life, the daily walks and drives, the annual migrations to Scotland and back, it was an event of rare, spontaneous, gaiety.

Beatrice was twenty-seven when, in another departure from routine, instead of going to Osborne in the spring of 1884 Queen Victoria went to Hesse-Darmstadt for a wedding. The bride, Princess Victoria of Hesse, was the daughter of Alice who had died in 1878; the Queen felt a special responsibility for this motherless granddaughter, which was one reason why she went to the

Princess Beatrice in her wedding dress that was admired in the papers as 'a model of elegant simplicity'. She had had to fight for her mother's approval to her marriage. The Queen, whose own marriage had been so successful, was quite prepared to ask her daughter to forego the chance of equal happiness in order to remain as a companion in her old age.

wedding in person. Beatrice, the Queen's constant companion for the last thirteen years, naturally accompanied her.

Princess Victoria was marrying Prince Louis of Battenberg (the eldest child of this union was to become the mother of the present Duke of Edinburgh; the youngest child, Earl Mountbatten of Burma), one of four handsome, able brothers before whose collective and considerable charms the princesses of the royal houses of Europe went down like the proverbial ninepins. Beatrice was enamoured of Henry. The Battenbergs were attractive, but in royal circles,

Beatrice and Prince Henry of Battenberg, known in the family as Liko, on their wedding day; photograph by W. and D. Downey. The marriage was a controversial one, but once the Queen had been won over, she became the couple's staunchest champion.

controversial. Their father, Prince Alexander of Hesse, had fallen in love with a Polish Countess who was not royal. The only way to marry her had been morganatically, whereby he renounced the right to pass on to their children any titles or property. His wife had later been created Princess of Battenberg, and their children took this title as a family name. However, it cut no ice among families like the Prussian Hohenzollerns who jealously guarded the purity of ancestral bloodlines. When Prince Alexander of Battenberg requested the hand of Princess Victoria of Prussia, his 'impertinence' raised a storm in Berlin. Her family could not allow the match for reasons of rank, and Bismarck, Chancellor of Germany, for its political ramifications.

Beatrice fared better, though she had to fight hard to win Liko, as Prince Henry was known from a childhood version of his nickname Henrico. Queen

Victoria was not prejudiced against him in person or because of his rank – her daughter Louise, after all, had not married royalty and Victoria's support of the Battenbergs was well known – she simply objected to a husband for Beatrice in principle. Marriage in general, she felt, ought to be avoided if at all possible, and marriage for Beatrice, on whom she relied so heavily, was out of the question.

Beatrice, however, might have lost her childish sparkle, but not an ounce of her determination. As a child she had once been told by her mother that she

was not to have any pudding as it was bad for her. 'But Baby likes it, my dear', she had replied, calmly helping herself. The Queen volleyed and thundered; 'what agonies, what despair'; Beatrice's wishes made her 'quite ill'; she would not hear of it, 'hoped against hope that it would not be!'[1] At length, when she saw that Beatrice was so determined that her health would suffer, and also how badly hit she was by the premature death of her brother Leopold, to whom she had always been very close, the Queen relented. On condition that the couple remain with her under her roof, she would give her consent.

During the Christmas festivities of 1884, matters reached a convoluted point at which the suitor was made aware that the mother would not refuse him if he asked permission to request her daughter's hand; the Court watched developments with interest, as Sir Henry Ponsonby remarked to his wife:

Osborne House on the wedding day, *Illustrated London News*, 1 August 1885. As on so many occasions, the house was not big enough to hold all the guests, and marquees had to be put up on the lawn.

'Henry Battenberg comes to stay with his brother at Kent House on Tuesday next. Ahem!'[2] The Queen saw to it that the little drama of proposal and acceptance paid due homage to the household gods of Osborne:

I let Liko know, to come up after tea. I saw him in dear Albert's room and took his hand, which he kissed [sic], thanking me so much for what I had said. I told him what a struggle it had been for me, as Beatrice and I were so bound up in each other. Then I called in the dear child, and after holding their hands, and giving them my blessing, I left them to speak to each other.[3]

As well as winning his princess, the successful suitor melted the dragon: she was very soon writing that he was 'so nice, quite like one of ourselves, so gentle and quiet, in no way putting himself forward.'[4] As she explained, 'it is really

Liko himself who has won my heart. He is so modest, so full of consideration for me.' The couple were so 'quietly and really sensibly happy'; and the Queen was much relieved that there was none of the 'kissing etc.', which had so tried her with other daughters.[5]

The marquee arranged for the wedding breakfast (*above right*). A few hours after this feast, the guests were presented with an equally spectacular dinner (*above left*).

Between handing out Christmas presents to the servants, showing Liko all over Osborne, peeping through a door at the Punch and Judy show she had arranged as a birthday treat for Arthur's children, discussing Beatrice's trousseau and future accommodation at Osborne, and agonizing over the plight of General Gordon besieged in Khartoum, the Queen received a broadside of attacks from Berlin; the Hohenzollerns had just seen off one Battenberg; did the Queen realize what she was doing allowing his brother in? She refused to swallow such 'affronts': 'if the Queen of England thinks a person good enough for her daughter what have other people got to say?'[6] She nailed her colours to the mast and declared Liko the handsomest of the three handsome brothers. Perhaps such support of Beatrice's future husband was to repay her youngest daughter for her continuing loyalty: Queen Victoria was never half-hearted.

It was decided almost immediately that the wedding would take place at Whippingham Church. This did not follow the precedent of Princess Louise and the Marquess of Lorne who had married at Windsor, and on the face of it there was no reason why Princess Beatrice and Prince Henry of Battenberg could not have done likewise; but the controversial Battenberg background may have tipped the balance in favour of a 'quiet' parish wedding to which it would not be necessary to invite representatives of disapproving German reigning dynasties.

The Queen left Osborne as usual in the middle of February, and did not return until a few days before the wedding, which was set for 23 July 1885. Meanwhile, instructions and counter instructions flew by telegraph between Windsor and the Isle of Wight. When the Queen arrived she found that preparations were well ahead; a huge tent had already been put up on the lawn outside the Household dining room, and others near the kitchens. Soon another sprang up, connected to the Pavilion by a covered way. All the different arrangements, said the Queen, seemed excellent, and she found time to inspect the Camel Corps, with a lump in her throat at the memory of the bloody end of the siege of Khartoum.

Beatrice's trousseau of elegant dinner dresses, stylish costumes and 'dainty yachting gowns' was ready, down to the crimson silk stockings made and presented by the girls of the Soldiers' Daughters Home; the billiard room at Osborne 'quite filled' with presents, even though the largest had had to be left at Windsor; the bridegroom arrived looking 'well and ardent';[7] a forest of pot plants and flowers appeared in the hall, staircase, and tents; the people of Liverpool sent an enormous wedding cake on a silver tray ('Really the loyalty and kindness of the people is very great'[8]); wedding guests arrived to stay at Osborne House, Norris Castle and all the hotels, overflowing into the yachts in Osborne Bay and Cowes Roads. The pews were taken out of the church and the floor boarded over so that there were no steps; organist and choristers were imported from Windsor. The night before the wedding there was a vast family dinner in the tent outside the Pavilion. Beatrice wore one of her trousseau dresses and the rubies which, collected and arranged by Albert many years earlier, formed part of the Queen's wedding present to her.

The wedding day dawned fine and warm. Guests travelling down from London left Victoria by special train at nine o'clock. Beatrice and the Queen breakfasted alone together under the trees and saw Liko for a few minutes – the Queen did not miss the opportunity to issue more presents: a pin for him and a ruby half-hoop ring for her, which had been a gift to the Queen from her uncle the Duke of Sussex at her own marriage.

As the travelling guests boarded the *Alberta*, waiting for them at Portsmouth, Beatrice began to dress for her wedding, just as Alice had done twenty-three years before, in Albert's room. She went to the altar with her buxom figure corseted in symbolism. The veil had been the Queen's own wedding veil, which Victoria had subsequently worn at all her children's christenings and lastly at Leopold's wedding; the diamond circlet and the stars that crowded in her hair were part of the Queen's wedding present; and the ivory white satin dress was trimmed with the Queen's wedding lace. She was all set about with sprays of meaningful flowers: orange blossom, traditional for weddings; white heather, no doubt from the hills of Balmoral; and myrtle, plucked, of an equal certainty, from one of the dynastic bushes in the grounds of Osborne. Her dress was very long, but as the wedding was to be a 'simple' affair in a parish church she wore no train. A Guard of Honour of the 93rd Highlanders with their band, played her off from the house; the Isle of Wight Volunteers were drawn up at the gate and all along the road to Whippingham the way was lined with cheering crowds. 'She did look so sweet', thought the Queen, sitting opposite her in the carriage.[9]

They reached the church at one o'clock where they found Bertie, and a flock of ten bridesmaid princesses wearing white dresses, long white gloves, white stockings, and white shoes with little bows on the front, carrying bouquets of red and white carnations that matched the flowers pinned to their dresses. They were all nieces of the bride, among them three Victorias, as well as the future Queens of Norway and Romania, and the beautiful melancholy Princess Alix of Hesse, who was to be the last Tsarina of Russia.

The bridesmaids lined up behind their aunt in pairs, smallest last. The Lord Chamberlain and the Lord Steward took up their places at the front of the procession; the Queen, in a sumptuous black dress of *broché grenadine*, woven to a floral design which had exercised all the art of the Lyons silk-weavers, walked on one side of the bride, Bertie on the other. To the strains of Wagner's 'Brant Chor' from *Lohengrin*, they advanced up the red carpet, laid along the covered way which had been put up specially, the roof and columns all draped with red and white, between admiring rows of people, and into the church crammed with guests. The 'brilliant, festive effect' was just to the Queen's taste: 'imposing, though simple'.[10]

At the altar waited Prince Henry, with his flaring moustaches, in the spectacular white uniform of the Garde du Corps of the Prussian Household Cavalry, with gleaming boots and spurs. Around his neck was the Order of the Garter which the Queen had conferred on him a few days previously. The Archbishop of Canterbury, the Bishop of Winchester, the Dean of Windsor, and Canon Prothero from Whippingham officiated, and the service went just as the Queen would have wished it. She had been present at all her children's weddings except Affie's; and she watched this ceremony with more composure than any of the others: 'A happier looking couple could seldom be seen kneeling at the altar together. It was very touching. I stood close to my dear child, who looked very sweet, pure, and calm.'[11]

In the carriage on the way back, driving between crowds who cheered, if possible, even louder than before, the Queen spared a thought for Alice. Victoria had come a long way since the last woeful Osborne wedding under the Family Picture. Now, though this icon still hung where it always had, the dining room did not feature in the ceremonies at all, except as a passage.

On arriving home they went straight into the drawing room for the signing of the register which the Dean of Windsor had brought from the Chapel Royal. Beatrice and Liko signed first, then the Queen, then both families. The order of signing on these occasions had in the past been the cause of many unseemly wrangles, so in this case it had been determined in advance, and approved by

Princess Beatrice and Prince Henry of Battenberg surrounded by their attendants. From left to right: (back row) Alexander, Prince of Bulgaria, Princess Louise of Wales, Princess Irene of Hesse, Princess Victoria of Wales, Prince Franz Josef of Battenberg; (middle row) Princess Maud of Wales, Princess Alix of Hesse, Princess Marie Louise and Princess Helena Victoria of Schleswig-Holstein; (front row) Princess Victoria Melita, Princess Marie and Princess Alexandra of Edinburgh.

the Queen. Only the bride and groom, and three or four witnesses signed the Whippingham register.

Beatrice, Liko and the Queen took up their positions opposite the door, and all the wedding guests filed past, and out into the gardens. The Queen would have been able to distinguish which of the ladies had travelled to the island for the day, as they had been permitted to come in bonnets and smart morning dresses; ladies who were staying on the island wore demi-toilette evening dresses with bodies cut down at the back, elbow-length sleeves, and jewels in their hair, as though for a full dress evening party; men wore levée dress.

Over sixty royalty sat down in the tent beside the Pavilion for the wedding breakfast. Two bands played, and the ten pipers of the Sutherland and Argyll Highlanders marched round the table, 'playing splendidly together', noted the Queen. Gilded menu cards, adorned with dangling cherubs, swags of myrtle, coats of arms, and a portrait of Osborne, set out the feast of seven courses, with twenty-two separate dishes. A consommé such as that which opened the proceedings, decorated with tiny quenelles that melted in the mouth, took three days to prepare; and no less care would have been expended on the cream soup. Then came three hot 'entrées': lamb cutlets decorated with artichokes and an elegant tomato sauce; fillets of chicken (at that time an opulent delicacy), richly embellished with truffles; and breasts of duckling with peas. These were removed by capons and fillets of beef.

The cold entrées to tempt both the eye and the palate followed: salad dressed *à la Parisienne*, pheasants glazed with aspic *à la bellevue*, (the ancestry of this dish deriving from the days when Madame Pompadour devised titillations for the capricious appetite of Louis XIV), domes of chicken mayonnaise, and lobster salad. Next came a display from the roasting cooks: chicken, and the last word in luxury, roast ortolans, a kind of bunting so small they only needed five or six minutes on the roasting spit and were eaten whole, bones and all. Pudding *à la diplomate* gave way to the entremets, a course consisting of vegetables and sweet dishes: peas sautéed in butter, spinach in a velouté sauce, 'les gelées de mosaiques', and an array of meringues, génoises, babas, and mocha gâteaux which showed off the arts of the patisserie cooks.

Every single mouthful had had to make the normal journey along the basement passages from the kitchen to the tabledeckers' room then, instead of going upstairs to the dining room, it had all been carried round the Pavilion basement area, up a specially-constructed staircase, over the area balustrade of the Pavilion and into the tent.[12]

All the royalties were taken onto the terrace after lunch for the wedding photographs; then Beatrice went up to change her dress for a cream-coloured crêpe de Chine, trimmed with lace, and a toque with a spray of white heather, orange blossom and myrtle. Liko had changed out of his uniform, and had swapped his gleaming helmet with its flying eagle for a smart grey top hat. The Queen was finally overcome; she could not go down to see them off, and sobbed bitterly when they had gone, hearing in the distance the band playing and the crowds cheering as the couple set out for Quarr Abbey where they were to spend their honeymoon.

The Queen spent the rest of the afternoon much as she usually did, answering telegrams, taking a turn in the carriage, and out on the lawn for tea.

A family group at Osborne, photograph by Hughes & Mullins, August 1887. From left to right: Mohamed Bukhsh; Abdul Karim; Princess Marie of Edinburgh; Arthur, Duke of Connaught; Princess Beatrice and Princess Victoria Melita of Edinburgh; Queen Victoria; Beatrice, Princess Henry of Battenberg (back view); Stephen Maslin; Princess Alix and Princess Irene of Hesse; nurse with Prince Alexander of Battenberg, Beatrice's eldest child.

As she was dressing for dinner she received a comforting note from Beatrice to say that they had reached the Abbey safely. As though the feast which had been laid before them a few hours earlier had never been, Queen Victoria and her guests sat down to a six-course dinner. It was a state occasion, at which the men wore uniform; and a similar grandeur was reflected in the menu. The healths of the Queen, the bride and bridegroom, and Liko's parents, were proposed, and drunk. The yachts in the bay lit up and sent off rockets and the band played on the lower terrace, but the Queen was too tired to stay long; she escaped quietly to her room, thinking of her 'dear child'. Marriage, the Queen was inclined to think, was a trap, sprung upon unsuspecting brides who, if they were allowed to go to the altar in the full knowledge of what was in store for them, might never go up the aisle at all.

Her fears were groundless. Beatrice's 'trap' brought the young wife great happiness, and very soon the Queen had banished regret when she discovered that she herself was enjoying this late, reflected sunshine. Before long, new grandchildren began arriving. Henry and Beatrice had three sons and a daughter, and the Queen thoroughly enjoyed them: 'Beatrice's sweet little baby, is brought down to me every evening after his bath, and looks too delightful in his nightgown.'[13] As they grew older, they would be brought into her room at tea time every evening, and play 'quite happily' on the floor, looked after by one of the Queen's Indian attendants. Once again, the Queen went everywhere accompanied by a nursery and what her Private Secretary called a 'cloud' of nurses.[14] The inevitable accidents and illnesses of childhood, taking place under her own roof, would make her exclaim 'I love these darling children so, almost as much as their own parents.'[15] Some of the lost magic of Christmas returned.

As though reflecting this new dimension in the Queen's life, and her acceptance of change, the shape of Osborne House itself altered, and the Queen added a new wing to the Pavilion. Albert had designed Osborne for himself and his young family. There was not really enough room for another family, nor was there a single room large enough for the huge gatherings over which the elderly Queen presided. For years, major events at Osborne had had to take place under canvas. This ad hoc state of affairs came to an end in 1890, when a new wing was built on to the Pavilion: 'it looks quite strange, but it will be an improvement and a great advantage', commented the Queen,[16] who had hesitated for so long over the addition of so much as a single wall to Osborne, being, as she had once written, 'always in doubt when it comes *to the point, — being so afraid to meddle with or spoil what the dear Prince had planned and built.*'[17]

Several members of the family contributed ideas to the new wing. The Queen was grateful to Louise for taking so much trouble over the plans; Beatrice was glad to have a suite of rooms for herself and her family; and through Arthur, the Queen commissioned Bhai Ram Singh, of the Mayo School of Art in Lahore, to design the elaborate Indian plasterwork decoration for the new dining room, which became known as the Durbar Room. Too late, Vicky suggested that the exterior of the new wing would have looked better if the colonnade had been continued along it. Without Albert's unifying vision the new wing, an imperial postscript, sat awkwardly on Albert's Italianate house. Nevertheless, the Durbar Room was very successful, as dining room, present room (at Christmas), and theatre, where Twelfth Night could be celebrated with plays and tableaux vivants.

Prince Henry's vigorous presence injected new life into the staid amusements of an elderly Court, and dinner was a dull affair when the Battenbergs were not dining downstairs. Prince Henry was also a keen sportsman. 'He is passionately fond of the sea', observed the Queen, as he raced his yacht, the *Leander*, during Cowes Week.[18] Even that most reluctant of sailors, Sir Henry

OSBORNE

Her Majesty's Dinner.

Christmas Day, 1896.

Potages.
La Tête de Veau En Tortue.   Aux trois racines.

Poissons.
Le Turbot bouilli sauce hollandaise.
Les Filets de soles frits.

Entrée.
Les Kromeskys à la Toulouse.

Relevés.
Les Dindes rôties à la Chipolata.
Chine of Pork.
Rt Sirloin of Beef.   Plum Pudding.

Entremets.
Les Asperges sauce mousseline.
Mince Pies.
Le Pain de riz à la cintra.

Side Table.

Baron of Beef.   Woodcock Pie.   Brawn.
Wild Boar's Head.   Game Pie.

Ponsonby, found himself compelled aboard His Royal Highness's cutter. Prince Henry's powers of persuasion must have been considerable; for he even prevailed upon the Queen to allow him to ride to hounds, which she had always considered dangerous (and had disliked Albert doing). Prince Henry and Beatrice took an active role in the official life of the Isle of Wight. In 1885 he became the first Honorary Colonel of the 5th Volunteer Battalion of the Hampshire Regiment and in 1890 he was appointed Governor of the Isle of Wight.

The conditions, however, upon which the Queen had allowed the marriage, had condemned Prince Henry to the very situation, virtually that of

OPPOSITE: A decorative menu for Her Majesty's dinner, Christmas Day 1896.

permanent guest in someone else's house, which Albert, fifty years earlier, had solved by building Osborne. Prince Henry's escape from an unfulfilling satellite role took him to West Africa, during the Ashanti War of 1895–6, where he contracted malaria. He died on the way home, and was buried at Whippingham. Beatrice's happiness was cruelly cut short, but she bore her loss with great stoicism. The Queen mourned with her, echoing a phrase she had once used about Albert: 'He was the bright sunshine of our Home.'[19] Once again, there was 'such an awful blank and stillness everywhere'.[20] Nevertheless the old Queen was able to balance grief with acceptance at 'dear lovely Osborne, with its sunshine, lovely flowers, soft air and all its bright as well as sad associations.'[21]

With the Queen in the gardens at Osborne in 1898 are three future kings: the bearded sailor who became George V, holding the boy who would be George VI; and the future Edward VIII in a sailor suit (third from the left).

POSTSCRIPT

In January 1901 Queen Victoria died at Osborne. The only sound at the end of a great reign was the fountain on the terrace below, a sound at once soothing and melancholy. Edward VII and the Kaiser lifted her into her coffin on top of the strange collection of talismanic objects which she had directed should go to the grave with her, and she was taken downstairs to the dining room where she lay in state for several days before beginning her last journey to join her beloved husband in the mausoleum at Frogmore. Although so many of the royal children had spent happy times at Osborne, none of them took it on. Edward VII preferred the more accessible pleasures of Sandringham; his son was unwilling to embark on the expense of keeping up such a large house, and none of the King's sisters could afford it. The King solved his problem by giving the house to the nation by an Act of Parliament of 1902. The Main and Household Wings became a convalescent home for officers, whilst part of the ground floor was opened to the public. The royal family's own apartments remained largely unaltered. The Queen's bedroom became a *chapelle ardente*, or mortuary chapel, and only visited by members of the family. The best paintings were copied and the originals taken to Buckingham Palace or Windsor. Much of the furniture – other than the pieces in the Pavilion – was too large to be suitable for other royal residences and was sold off. The Durbar Room became a museum. The Council Room, where sometimes the Queen had danced, and sometimes held council, became the officers' mess and the gilded ceilings dimmed under the smoke from their cigarettes and pipes. The estate was broken up and sold off. In 1955, by permission of Her Majesty The Queen, the private apartments were opened to the public. Today, ninety years after the death of Queen Victoria, the Edward VII Convalescent Home is run by the Civil Service Benevolent Fund, while English Heritage manage the state apartments, which are being carefully restored; these are, once more, as Prince Albert created them.

Osborne House as it is today. The terraces and royal apartments remain very much as the Prince Consort left them.

REFERENCE NOTES

For full bibliographical details of works
cited see p. 203.

Abbreviations
PP Osb.: Privy Purse, Osborne
RA: Royal Archives, Windsor Castle
Remarks: Queen Victoria, Remarks –
  Conversations – Reflections
Reminiscences: Queen Victoria's
  Reminiscences, 1840–1861
QVJ: Queen Victoria's Journal

CHAPTER ONE

The First Years of Marriage

1. RA QVJ, 10 October 1839.
2. Queen Victoria to the Princess Royal,
   9 June 1858; quoted in Fulford (ed.),
   Dearest Child.
3. Queen Victoria to King Leopold,
   7 June 1836; RA Y88/15.
4. Queen Victoria to King Leopold,
   15 July 1839; RA Y89/41.
5. RA QVJ, 11 October 1839.
6. Lyttelton, 1912, p. 298.
7. Queen Victoria to Prince Albert,
   31 January 1840; RA Z490/23.
8. Queen Victoria to Stockmar, 20
   January 1842; RA Add. U2/8.
9. Queen Victoria to the Princess Royal,
   8 March 1858; quoted in Fulford,
   op. cit., p. 72.
10. Lyttelton, 1912, p. 300.
11. Queen Victoria to King Leopold,
    16 January 1844; RA Y91/35.
12. RA QVJ, 19 October 1843.
13. Queen Victoria, Memorandum,
    10 May 1878; RA PP Osb. 564.
14. RA QVJ, 21 December 1880.
15. Prince Albert to Sir Robert Peel;
    19 February 1844; RA F21/20.
16. Report on Osborne, 4 December
    1844; RA F21/11.
17. RA QVJ, 15 October 1844.

18. Prince Albert, Memorandum on
    Osborne, 21 October 1844; RA
    F21/53.
19. RA F21/94.
20. RA QVJ, 12 April 1844.
21. Queen Victoria to King Leopold,
    25 March 1845; RA Y92/16.
22. Stanley, *Twenty Years at Court*, p. 28.

CHAPTER TWO

The Creation of Osborne

1. RA F21/53.
2. RA QVJ, 31 March 1845.
3. RA QVJ, 29 March 1845.
4. RA PP Osb. 2.
5. RA QVJ, 12 May 1845.
6. RA QVJ, 15 May 1845.
7. RA QVJ, 20 June 1845.
8. Prince Albert to Caroline, Duchess of
   Saxe-Gotha-Altenburg, 24 June
   1845; RA M35/73.
9. RA QVJ, 23 June 1845.
10. RA QVJ, 23 July 1845.
11. RA QVJ, 25 July 1845.
12. RA QVJ, 20 August 1845.
13. RA QVJ, 10 September 1845.
14. *The Illustrated London News*, 13
    December 1845, no. 189, vol. VII,
    p. 381.
15. Queen Victoria, Memorandum,
    22 February 1874; RA Y169/89.
16. RA QVJ, 28 December 1863.
17. Quoted in Surtees, *Charlotte Canning*,
    p. 170.
18. RA QVJ, 25 November 1845.
19. RA QVJ, 30 November 1845.
20. RA QVJ, 25 November 1845.
21. RA QVJ, 14 July 1846.
22. RA QVJ, 1 September 1846.
23. Hobhouse, *Thomas Cubitt*, p. 538,
    note 40.
24. RA QVJ, 14 September 1846.
25. Ibid.

26. Ibid.
27. Ibid.
28. Lyttelton, 1873, p. 376.
29. RA QVJ, 16 September 1846.
30. RA QVJ, 17 September 1846.
31. RA QVJ, 18 September 1846.
32. RA QVJ, 1 December 1845.
33. RA QVJ, 3 March 1846.
34. RA QVJ, 22 November 1851.
35. Lyttelton, 1873, p. 380.
36. RA QVJ, 18 November 1846.
37. RA QVJ, 3 March 1847.
38. RA QVJ, 7 May 1847.
39. RA QVJ, 9 December 1846.
40. RA QVJ, 30 July 1847.
41. RA QVJ, 31 July 1847.
42. Lyttelton, 1912, p. 368.
43. RA QVJ, 29 September 1847.
44. Stanley, *Twenty Years at Court*, p. 167.
45. RA QVJ, 4 December 1847.
46. RA QVJ, 26 November 1847.
47. RA QVJ, 20 December 1847.
48. RA QVJ, 10 December 1851.
49. Stanley, op. cit., p. 166.
50. Reminiscences, p. 13; RA Z491.
51. Stanley, op. cit., p. 167
52. 12 October 1849; RA PP Osb. 39.
53. RA QVJ, 13 July 1849.
54. RA QVJ, 23 November 1849.
55. Andrew Toward, Letter, 12 January
    1850; RA PP Osb. 41.
56. RA QVJ, 1 August 1849.
57. RA QVJ, 17 March 1849.
58. RA QVJ, 19 December 1849.
59. RA QVJ, 24 November 1849.
60. RA QVJ, 26 July 1852.
61. RA QVJ, 8 August 1852.
62. RA QVJ, 12 August 1884.
63. RA QVJ, 3 March 1849.
64. RA Z141/39.
65. RA QVJ, 30 March 1845.
66. RA QVJ, 20 December 1848.
67. RA QVJ, 9 March 1849.
68. RA PP Osb. 564.

69. Queen Victoria to Sir Thomas Biddulph, 8 February 1873; RA Z204/16.

CHAPTER THREE

A Place of One's Own

1. RA QVJ, 23 May 1854.
2. RA QVJ, 19 May 1860.
3. Queen Victoria to the Princess Royal, 5 December 1859; quoted in Fulford (ed.), *Dearest Child*, p. 222.
4. RA QVJ, 1 October 1849.
5. RA QVJ, 16 May 1857.
6. RA QVJ, 26 May 1853.
7. Quoted in Kennedy (ed.), *My Dear Duchess*, p. 106.
8. RA M13/67.
9. Sir Howard Elphinstone, Diary, 8 December 1859; RA Add. A25/819.
10. RA QVJ, 9 March 1860.
11. Prince Albert to the Princess Royal, 1 September 1850; quoted in Jagow (ed.), *Letters of the Prince Consort*, p. 311.
12. Queen Victoria to Vicky, 11 June 1858; quoted in Hibbert (ed.), *Queen Victoria in her Letters and Journals*, p. 105.
13. RA QVJ, 13 August 1858.
14. RA QVJ, 18 July 1854.
15. 'He could not bear bad manners, and always dealt out his dear reprimands to the juveniles – a word from him was instantly obeyed.' Reminiscences; RA Z491.
16. RA QVJ, 8 March 1860.
17. Lyttelton, 1873, p. 446.
18. Reminiscences, p. 17a; RA Z491.
19. RA QVJ, 12 March 1847.
20. Stanley, *Twenty Years at Court*, p. 362.
21. RA QVJ, 25 July 1853.
22. RA QVJ, 18 August 1854.
23. RA QVJ, 21 March 1858.
24. RA QVJ, 21 May 1858.
25. Reminiscences, p. 165; RA Z491.
26. Catherine Paget, 18 January 1868; RA Add.X136, p. 2.
27. Queen Victoria, Memorandum, *c.* 6 July 1880; RA PP Osb. 557.
28. RA PP Osb. 719.
29. John Mann to Captain Fleetwood Edwards, 3 July 1880; RA PP Osb. 557.
30. Letters of Frieda Arnold; RA Add.U291, translation, p. 5/2. Copyright Heinrich C. Weltzien, Bonn, Germany.
31. Patchett-Martin, 'The Queen in the Isle of Wight', p. 32.

32. Frieda Arnold; op. cit.
33. Emma Wallis, Diary, 1865–6; RA Add.X2/211, p. 149–50.
34. RA QVJ, 22 November 1851.
35. Emma Wallis; op. cit., p. 102.

CHAPTER FOUR

Life in the Royal Nursery

1. RA QVJ, 19 June 1845.
2. RA QVJ, 21 July 1845.
3. Reminiscences; RA Z491.
4. Lady Lyttelton to Queen Victoria, 8 August [1845]; RA M13/65.
5. Lady Lyttelton, Journal, 22–25 August [1845]; RA M13/68.
6. Ibid.
7. Ibid.
8. Lady Lyttelton, Journal, 26–28 August [1845]; RA M13/70.
9. Lady Lyttelton to Queen Victoria, 18 August [1845]; RA M13/87.
10. RA QVJ, 3 March 1846.
11. RA QVJ, 11 July 1846.
12. RA QVJ, 30 June 1846.
13. RA QVJ, 13 July 1846.
14. RA QVJ, 18 July 1846.
15. Lyttelton, 1873, p. 374.
16. RA QVJ, 14 September 1846.
17. RA QVJ, 22 November 1846.
18. RA QVJ, 6 December 1846.
19. RA QVJ, 14 December 1846.
20. RA QVJ, 22 November 1846.
21. RA QVJ, 1 August 1847.
22. RA QVJ, 2 December 1847.
23. RA QVJ, 3 October 1847.
24. Lyttelton, 1873, p. 407.
25. Ibid., p. 411.
26. Ibid.
27. Ibid., p. 408.
28. Ibid., p. 423.
29. Ibid., p. 412.
30. RA QVJ, 4 December 1848.
31. RA QVJ, 19 December 1848.
32. RA QVJ, 25 May 1860.
33. RA QVJ, 1 May 1853.
34. Lyttelton, 1873, p. 405.
35. RA QVJ, 18 March 1859.
36. RA QVJ, 1 May 1853.
37. RA QVJ, 25 May 1858.
38. RA QVJ, 1 May 1853.
39. RA QVJ, 25 May 1853.
40. RA QVJ, 18 March 1852.
41. RA QVJ, 25 May 1860.
42. RA QVJ, 25 May 1853.
43. Ibid.
44. RA QVJ, 27 May 1853.
45. RA QVJ, 26 November 1853.
46. RA QVJ, 18 July 1854.
47. RA QVJ, 15 May 1856.
48. RA QVJ, 27 August 1859.

49. Princess Alice to the Prince Consort, 29 May 1858; RA M19/34.
50. Madame Rollande de la Sauge to Mrs Isabella Tylor, 27 May [1857]; RA Add.C8/13.
51. RA QVJ, 27 May 1850.
52. RA PP Osb. 490–494,
53. RA QVJ, 24 July 1857.
54. Princess Alice to the Prince Consort, 19 August 1858; RA M19/38.
55. Ibid., 29 May 1858; RA M19/34.
56. Princess Louise to the Prince Consort, 3 June [1858]; RA M19/54.
57. Princess Helena to the Prince Consort, 28 May 1858; RA M19/40.
58. Prince Leopold to the Prince Consort, 1858; RA M19/67.
59. Vicky to Bertie, 13 December 1855; RA Add.A4/248.

CHAPTER FIVE

The Happiest Years

1. RA QVJ, 20 December 1849.
2. RA QVJ, 28 November 1849.
3. RA QVJ, 26 August 1854.
4. RA QVJ, 26 August 1853.
5. RA QVJ, 26 August 1856.
6. Anon., *Catalogue of the Paintings, Sculpture and other Works of Art at Osborne*, p. 61.
7. RA QVJ, 26 August 1850.
8. RA QVJ, 26 August 1852.
9. RA QVJ, 26 August 1857.
10. RA QVJ, 26 August 1859.
11. RA QVJ, 26 August 1854.
12. RA QVJ, 16 January 1845.
13. RA QVJ, 26 August 1850.
14. RA QVJ, 26 August 1850.
15. Ibid.
16. Ibid.
17. RA QVJ, 18 July 1854.
18. RA QVJ, 13 December 1853.
19. RA QVJ, 26 August 1856.
20. RA QVJ, 26 August 1852.
21. Ibid.
22. RA QVJ, 26 August 1854.
23. RA QVJ, 27 August 1851.
24. Lady Lyttelton to Queen Victoria, 26 August 1849; RA M13/100.
25. *The Illustrated London News*, 5 September 1846, no. 227, vol. IX, p. 148.
26. RA QVJ, 29 August 1846.
27. Lyttelton, 1912, p. 391.
28. RA QVJ, 24 May 1853.
29. Ibid.
30. RA QVJ, 24 May 1852.
31. RA QVJ, 24 May 1849.
32. RA QVJ, 24 May 1854.
33. RA QVJ, 24 May 1856.

34. Ibid.
35. Ibid.
36. RA QVJ, 24 May 1853.
37. RA QVJ, 24 May 1857.
38. Ibid.
39. RA QVJ, 24 May 1849.
40. RA QVJ, 24 May 1854.
41. RA QVJ, 24 May 1850.
42. RA QVJ, 24 May 1854.
43. RA QVJ, 14 August 1851.
44. RA QVJ, 5 August 1850.
45. RA QVJ, 18 August 1851.
46. Ibid.
47. RA QVJ, 5 August 1850.
48. RA QVJ, 24 November 1851.
49. RA QVJ, 20 December 1851.
50. RA QVJ, 3 December 1851.
51. RA QVJ, 11 August 1853.
52. Ibid.
53. Ibid.
54. RA QVJ, 18 August 1853.
55. Ibid.
56. RA QVJ, 11 March 1854.
57. Ibid.
58. Ibid.
59. Ibid.
60. RA QVJ, 6 January 1855.
61. RA QVJ, 5 August 1854.
62. RA QVJ, 15 March 1855.
63. RA QVJ, 28 May 1855.
64. RA QVJ, 24 July 1855.
65. RA QVJ, 20 July 1855.
66. RA QVJ, 29 July 1855.
67. RA QVJ, 13 August 1855.
68. RA QVJ, 13 July 1855.
69. Ibid.
70. RA QVJ, 11 August 1855.
71. RA QVJ, 28 August 1855.
72. RA QVJ, 1 September 1855.
73. RA QVJ, 12 May 1856.
74. Ibid.
75. Ibid.
76. RA QVJ, 18 July 1856.
77. RA QVJ, 11 December 1856.
78. RA QVJ, 31 May 1857.
79. RA QVJ, 2 June 1857.
80. RA QVJ, 6 August 1857.
81. RA QVJ, 10 August 1857.
82. RA QVJ, 25 May 1856.
83. RA QVJ, 8 August 1857.
84. Ibid.
85. RA QVJ, 10 August 1857.
86. Ibid.
87. Ibid.
88. RA QVJ, 20 May 1858.
89. Prince Albert to Vicky, [1854]; RA M19/21.
90. Queen Victoria to Vicky, 31 May 1858; quoted in Fulford (ed.), *Dearest Child*, p. 110.

91. Prince Arthur to the Prince Consort, 31 May [?1858]; RA M19/60.
92. Ibid, 3 October 1860; RA M19/63.
93. RA QVJ, 25 May 1859.
94. RA QVJ, 12 July 1859.
95. Stanley, *Twenty Years at Court*, p. 363.
96. Reminiscences, p. 25; RA Z491.
97. RA QVJ, 3 April 1861.
98. RA QVJ, 4 April 1861.
99. RA QVJ, 25 April 1861.
100. RA QVJ, 17 April 1861.
101. RA QVJ, 6 August 1861.

CHAPTER SIX

Dear Desolate Osborne

1. Remarks, p. 221; RA Z261.
2. Ibid., p. 231.
3. Ibid., p. 215.
4. Ibid., p. 221.
5. RA QVJ, 26 February 1862.
6. RA QVJ, 3 February 1862.
7. Queen Victoria to Vicky, 8 January 1862; quoted in Fulford (ed.), *Dearest Mama*, p. 34.
8. Bolitho (ed.), *Letters of Lady Augusta Stanley*, p. 251.
9. RA QVJ, 5 January 1862.
10. Remarks, p. 234; RA Z261.
11. RA QVJ, 6 January 1862.
12. RA QVJ, 20 January 1862.
13. Charles Dickens to John Leech, 5 September 1864; *The Letters of Charles Dickens*, vol. III, 1858–70, edited by Walter Dexter (London, 1938), p. 397.
14. Stanley, *Twenty Years at Court*, p. 394.
15. John Mann to Sir Thomas Biddulph, 29 October 1864; RA PP Add.Vic. 2146.
16. Remarks, p. 232; RA Z261.
17. RA PP Osb. 624.
18. Queen Victoria to Andrew Blake, 28 December 1889; RA Z198/43.
19. RA QVJ, 24 January 1863.
20. RA QVJ, 17 April 1862.
21. Queen Victoria to Vicky, 2 July 1862; quoted in Fulford, op. cit., p. 85.
22. RA QVJ, 30 June 1862.
23. Remarks, p. 251; RA Z261.
24. Lady Churchill to Eleanor Stanley; quoted in Stanley, op. cit., p. 398.
25. Remarks, p. 252; RA Z261.
26. Ibid., p. 253.
27. Ibid.
28. Ibid., p. 255.
29. Ibid.
30. Queen Victoria to Vicky; quoted in Fulford, op. cit., p. 38.
31. Hon. Mrs Bruce to Col. Biddulph, 14 January 1863; RA PP Add.Vic. 1614.

32. Reminiscences, p. 15; RA Z491.
33. RA QVJ, 9 July 1863.
34. RA QVJ, 1 January 1862.
35. RA QVJ, 6 January 1863.
36. Remarks, p. 227; RA Z261.
37. RA QVJ, 6 January 1865.
38. RA QVJ, 7 May 1867.
39. Longford, *Victoria R.I.*, p. 325.
40. RA QVJ, 6 May 1865.
41. RA QVJ, 8 May 1865.
42. RA QVJ, 5 February 1864.
43. RA QVJ, 6 August 1863.
44. RA QVJ, 25 April 1864.
45. RA QVJ, 14 July 1864.
46. Emma Wallis, Diary, 1865–6; RA Add.X2/211, p. 142.
47. RA QVJ, 29 July 1873.
48. RA QVJ, 28 December 1866.
49. Hallé, p. 292–4.
50. Ibid., p. 296.
51. RA QVJ, 13 July 1866.

CHAPTER SEVEN

A New Page

1. Queen Victoria to the Crown Princess, 3 January 1885; quoted in Fulford (ed.), *Beloved Mama*, p. 177.
2. 19 December 1884; RA Add.A36.
3. RA QVJ, 29 December 1884.
4. RA QVJ, 5 January 1885.
5. Queen Victoria to the Crown Princess, 7 January 1885; quoted in Fulford, op. cit., p. 177.
6. Queen Victoria to the Crown Princess, 10 January 1885; ibid., pp. 178–9.
7. 20 July 1885; RA Add.A36.
8. RA QVJ, 15 July 1885.
9. RA QVJ, 23 July 1885.
10. Ibid.
11. Ibid.
12. PP Osb. 726.
13. RA QVJ, 24 July 1887.
14. Sir Henry Ponsonby, 29 December 1886; RA Add.A36.
15. RA QVJ, 10 February 1894.
16. RA QVJ, 18 July 1890.
17. Queen Victoria to Sir Henry Ponsonby, 19 August 1880; RA PP Osb. 539.
18. RA QVJ, 2 August 1886.
19. RA QVJ, 22 January 1896.
20. RA QVJ, 24 July 1896.
21. RA QVJ, 31 August 1896.

SELECT BIBLIOGRAPHY

AMES, WINSLOW, *Prince Albert and Victorian Taste*, London, 1967

ANON., *Catalogue of the Paintings, Sculpture, and other Works of Art at Osborne*, London, 1876

ANON., *Osborne House 1845–1890*, Newport, Isle of Wight, n.d.

ANON., *The Private Life of The Queen 1897; By One of Her Majesty's Servants*, Old Woking, 1979

BAIRD, DIANA (ed.), *Victorian Days and a Royal Friendship*, Worcester, 1958

BENNET, DAPHNE, *King Without a Crown: Albert, Prince Consort of England 1819–1861*, London, 1977

BENSON, ARTHUR CHRISTOPHER, and VISCOUNT ESHER, *The Letters of Queen Victoria; A Selection from Her Majesty's Correspondence between the Years 1837 and 1861*, London, 1907

BOLITHO, HECTOR, and the DEAN OF WINDSOR (eds.), *Letters of Lady Augusta Stanley: A Young Lady at Court*, London, 1927

DALHOUSIE LOGIN, E., *Lady Login's Recollections*, London, 1917

DIMOND, FRANCES, and TAYLOR, ROGER, *Crown and Camera; the Royal Family and Photography 1842–1910*, London, 1987

ERBACH-SCHÖNBERG, PRINCESS MARIE ZU, (Princess Battenberg), *Reminiscences*, London, 1925

FULFORD, ROGER (ed.), *Dearest Child, Letters between Queen Victoria and the Princess Royal, 1858–1861*, London, 1957

FULFORD, ROGER (ed.), *Dearest Mama; Letters between Queen Victoria and the Crown Princess of Prussia, 1861–1864*, London, 1968

FULFORD, ROGER (ed.), *Your Dear Letter, Private Correspondence of Queen Victoria and the Crown Princess of Prussia, 1865–1871*, London, 1971

GIROUARD, MARK, *The Victorian Country House*, London, 1979

HALLÉ, C. E. and HALLÉ, MARY (eds.), *The Life and Letters of Sir Charles Hallé*, London, 1896

HIBBERT, CHRISTOPHER (ed.), *Queen Victoria in her Letters and Journals*, London, 1984

HOBHOUSE, HERMIONE, *Thomas Cubitt, Master Builder*, London, 1971

HOBHOUSE, HERMIONE, *Prince Albert: His Life and Work*, London, 1983

JAGOW, KURT (ed.), *Letters of the Prince Consort, 1831–61*, London, 1938

KENNEDY, A. L. (ed.), *My Dear Duchess: Letters to the Duchess of Manchester 1858–1869*, London, 1956

LONGFORD, ELIZABETH, *Victoria R.I.*, London, 1982

LUTYENS, MARY (ed.), *Lady Lytton's Court Diary, 1875–1899*, London, 1961

LYTTELTON, LADY SARAH, *Letters from Sarah, Lady Lyttelton, 1797–1870*, London, 1873

LYTTELTON, LADY SARAH, *Correspondence of Sarah Spencer, Lady Lyttelton, 1787–1870*, edited by the Hon. Mrs Hugh Wyndham, London, 1912

MARIE OF ROUMANIA, *The Story of My Life*, New York, 1934

PATCHETT-MARTIN, A, 'The Queen in the Isle of Wight', *Vectis*, Brochure no. II, Shanklin, Isle of Wight, 1898

PONSONBY, ARTHUR, *Henry Ponsonby; Queen Victoria's Private Secretary: His Life From His Letters*, London, 1942

PONSONBY, MAGDALEN (ed.), *Mary Ponsonby: A Memoir, Some Letters and a Journal*, London, 1927

REID, MICHAELA, *Ask Sir James*, London, 1987

RHODES JAMES, ROBERT, *Albert, Prince Consort*, London, 1907

ROBERTS, JANE, *Royal Artists; From Mary Queen of Scots to the Present Day*, London, 1987

STANLEY, ELEANOR, *Twenty Years at Court*, London, 1916

SURTEES, VIRGINIA, *Charlotte Canning, Lady in Waiting to Queen Victoria and Wife of the First Viceroy of India 1817–1861*, London, 1976

WATSON, VERA, *A Queen at Home: An Intimate account of the Social and Domestic Life of Queen Victoria's Court*, London, 1952

WEINTRAUB, STANLEY, *Victoria, an Intimate Biography*, New York, 1987

WELLESLEY, COL. THE HON. F. A. (ed.), *The Paris Embassy during the Second Empire: Selections from the Papers of Henry Charles Wellesley, 1st Earl Cowley*, London, 1928

WOODHAM-SMITH, CECIL, *Queen Victoria Her Life and Times, vol. I, 1819–1861*, London, 1972

INDEX

Figures in italics refer to illustration captions. QV refers to Queen Victoria and PA to Prince Albert.

PICTURE
ACKNOWLEDGEMENTS

The author and publishers would like to thank the staff of the Royal Archives and Royal Library, Windsor, and the Royal Collection for their unfailing help in providing information and material for this book. The illustrations used are as follows: Reproduced by gracious permission of Her Majesty The Queen (copyright reserved) 2, 6, 14, 16, 17 (above), 18 (below), 19 (below), 21, 25, 26, 33, 37 (right), 38, 44, 53, 57, 62, 68, 70 (above), 70 (below), 73, 74, 76, 82, 83, 86, 88, 93, 94, 97 (left), 97 (right), 98, 99, 100, 101 (left), 101 (right), 105, 109, 110, 111, 112, 113, 114 (above), 115, 118, 119, 120 (left), 120 (right), 121, 122, 124, 128, 129, 130 (above), 130 (below), 131, 132, 135 (left), 135 (right), 138, 144, 146, 151, 152, 154, 155, 156, 160, 162, 164 (above), 164 (below), 165, 166, 170, 171, 173, 174, 175, 178, 179, 181, 183, 184, 186, 188 (left), 188 (right), 191, 193, 194, 195, 196, 197;

Windsor Castle, Royal Library © 1991 Her Majesty The Queen endpapers, 1, 17 (below), 18 (above), 19 (above), 20 (above), 20 (below), 22, 23 (above), 23 (below), 24, 27 (above left), 27 (above right), 27 (below), 28, 30, 31, 32, 34, 35, 36, 39, 40, 41, 42, 43, 45, 46, 49, 50 (above), 50 (below), 52, 54 (above), 54 (below), 56, 58, 59, 60 (below), 61, 64, 65, 66, 67, 69, 71, 72 (above), 72 (below), 75, 77, 78, 85, 89, 90, 91, 92, 95, 102, 103, 104, 106, 107, 108, 114 (below), 116, 126, 127, 133, 134, 136, 137, 139, 140, 142, 143, 145, 147, 150, 157 (left), 157 (above right), 157 (below right), 158, 159, 161, 176, 177, 182.

Acknowledgement and thanks are also due to the following museums and organizations for permission to reproduce pictures in their collections:
Reproduced by Courtesy of the Trustees of the British Museum 60 (above); Hillwood Museum, Washington, DC 148; The Illustrated London News Picture Library 37 (left), 55, 125, 187; Musée national du château de Compiègne © Photo R.M.N. 149; Royal Commission on the Historical Monuments of England 167, 169.

The following photographs were taken by Oliver Benn at Osborne House with the kind permission and assistance of English Heritage:
3 et al. (Coat of Arms from the Gibson Niche, Grand Corridor); 11 (Ceiling panel, Council Room); 15 (Door panel, Council Room); 29 (Door panel, Audience Room); 47; 63 (Ceiling panel, Billiard Room); 80; 81; 87 (Finger-plate, Council Room); 117 (Monogram from the Gibson Niche); 163 and 185 (Minton floor tiles, Grand Corridor); 198.